CHRISTIAN PUBLISHING HOUSE

HOW TO INTERPRET
THE BIBLE
An Introduction to Hermeneutics

Kieran Beville

HOW TO INTERPRET
THE BIBLE

An Introduction to Hermeneutics

Kieran Beville

Christian Publishing House
Cambridge, Ohio

Cover Image: Bede, The Venerable

Copyright © 2016 Kieran Beville

All rights reserved. Except for brief quotations in articles, other publications, book reviews, and blogs, no part of this book may be reproduced in any manner without prior written permission from the publishers. For information, write,

support@christianpublishers.org

Unless otherwise stated, Scripture quotations are from the English Standard Version (ESV) The Holy Bible, English Standard Version Copyright © 2001 by Crossway Bibles, a publishing ministry of Good News Publishers.

HOW TO INTERPRET THE BIBLE: An Introduction to Hermeneutics

ISBN-13: 978-1-945757-05-1

ISBN-10: 1-945757-05-1

INTERPRETING THE BIBLE

Kieran Beville

Table of Contents

Endorsements

In *How to Study the Bible* Kieran Beville explores how an understanding of hermeneutics enables a deeper engagement with the Scriptures. This well-written and thoughtful introduction will be a great asset to anyone wishing to see with greater clarity the revelation of God's heart and mind within the Bible. I warmly commend it. **(Dr Roger Standing, Principal, Spurgeon's College, London).**

CHAPTER 1 Preliminary Consideration

Anybody who wants to study the Bible, either at a personal level or at a more scholarly level needs to understand that there are certain principles that guide and govern the process. The technical word used to refer to the principles of biblical interpretation is *hermeneutics*. In a general sense, the word *hermeneutics* refers to the principles of textual interpretation. It is a methodological approach to textual analysis that applies to both secular and sacred texts. As such it forms the basis of literary criticism. Biblical hermeneutics is more specifically about the principles of biblical interpretation. It is of immense importance in Biblical Studies and Theology.

This work examines the principles of biblical interpretation by taking into consideration the cultural context, historical background and geographical location in which the text was originally set. This enables us to obtain clarity about the original author's intended meaning. Linguistic and literary factors are analyzed so that the various genres of Scripture are examined for their theological content.

Rationale

The importance of having good principles of interpretation cannot be overstated. To ignore them will result in all manner of erroneous assumptions. The aim of this work is to provide a sound and objective approach to the principles of biblical interpretation in order to provide a foundation for understanding and teaching Scripture. A proper hermeneutical approach will help avoid contradiction, inconsistency, arbitrariness, and subjectivity. Meanings or interpretations should not be based solely on personal wishes, feelings, or perceptions. Rather interpretations should be based on objective facts, reasons, and principles.

Objectives

This work aims to foster a deeper understanding of Scripture. It will help to develop an appreciation for the inspired and inerrant Word of God. It is designed to strengthen the conviction that Scripture has authority in all matters of faith and practice. This, in turn, should inspire faithfulness to the truth it teaches. As Christians are concerned not only with intellectual development but also with spiritual development, this work will help to cultivate a reverential appreciation for the divine nature of Scripture. It is intended to inspire greater confidence in the reliability and efficacy of Scripture and nurture humility in relation to scriptural knowledge. Because the Bible is a sacred text, the reader of Scripture is encouraged toward reliance on the Holy Spirit for illumination (in conjunction with scholarly endeavor). The reader of Scripture should have an attitude which is receptive and responsive to the revealed Word of God in terms of practical application. This work is intended for those who wish to develop a systematic and scholarly approach to biblical interpretation, especially those who wish to prepare teaching material grounded in safe hermeneutics.

Literal Interpretation

How literally should we understand Bible stories? Are the fall, the flood, Jonah, Job and other stories about real people and actual events? Are they metaphors for truth? Should we actually believe that two people ate a fruit and became estranged from God? Bible verses do not exist in isolation but as parts of larger units.

The Bible is self-consistent. In other words, it will not contradict itself. There is continuity in the storyline of the Bible. Is it descriptive or prescriptive? Is it specific to the occasion, or universal in application? What is central to the passage, and what are details only? The correct interpretation will be consistent with the historical-cultural background. What was the situation of the author and the audience?

The interpreter's job is to try to evaluate the original impact. How would the *Parable of The Good Samaritan* have impacted the original hearers? We also need to be able to take the interpretation from the ancient world and contextualize it for today. That means making it meaningful for people today. However, we must not allow culture to dictate how we interpret the Bible. Neither should "information" be the ultimate end of interpretation. The ultimate end of biblical interpretation is to understand its truth and to know God by entering into a deeper, dynamic relationship with him. This relationship begins with salvation and continues in an ongoing process of sanctification, which glorifies God through lives that are transformed by the living Word.

A proper understanding of the Word of God is essentially based on a literal interpretation - that is, according to the normal and plain sense of the written words. But everything in the Bible is not literal. There are non-literal, linguistic features such as metaphors and similes, allegories, parables, poetry, etc. A literal approach that allows for non-literal, linguistic features forms the foundation for a dependable understanding of doctrine.

Words have Meanings

Words have a range of meanings. We must determine which meaning of the word is most likely in the context we are examining. The same word will not be translated or interpreted the same way each time it is used. For example, In English, I might say: "He is green." The word "green" here can mean a number of things ~ such as "envious," "sick," "inexperienced" or "naïve." I probably intend only one of these meanings. Word meanings are not static; they change over time. This is evident in the English language. The word "gay" used to mean "merry" but now it is hardly ever used in that sense. It has come to mean something quite different in that it now relates to sexual identity in terms of orientation, attraction, and activity among members of the same sex. Similarly, the word "wicked" has taken on new meaning. It used to mean "very bad," "wrong" or "evil" but now it means the opposite ~ "very impressive." In English the King James Version (KJV) of the Bible uses the word "meat" for "food" but today the word "meat" refers to the flesh of animals.

Anachronisms

There is a danger of anachronistic readings when it comes to interpretation ~ that is imposing later meanings into earlier uses. The word "anachronism" comes from the Greek ανά (ana: up, against, back, re-) and χρόνος (chronos: time). It is a chronological inconsistency in some arrangement. It is something from a different period of time, placed in a historical setting. It is a chronological misplacing of persons, events, objects, or customs.

To properly interpret a passage we need to know what "language game" is being played. We need to know the rules which govern that game. Problems in interpretation will arise if we do not know which game we are playing. Problems in interpretation will arise if we use the wrong rules for a game.

A faith-Based Approach

A faith-based approach to the interpretation of Scripture presupposes that God has conveyed a message to humanity in the recorded words of the Bible. Literal interpretation recognizes the genre or textual design. That is, whether a passage is history, law, poetry, narrative, prophecy, apocalyptic, parable, epistle, gospel, etc. A correct genre judgment should be made to ensure correct understanding.

The historicity of a text must be affirmed in biblical narratives, which present themselves as factual. There may be a particular theological thrust to the selection and arrangement of data, but that does not negate its historicity. The biblical record of events and discourses may be presented in a variety of literary forms, but they correspond to historical fact and were not merely invented by the biblical writers.

The words of Scripture were originally conveyed in Hebrew, Greek, and Aramaic. But the Bible has been translated into many other languages and cultures. Transcendent truth is not bound by culture. Not every expression in another language will appropriately convey the original, intended meaning of Scripture. Thus, caution is needed so that the translators remain faithful to the truth of Scripture by the proper choice of words. All translation is an act of interpretation, whether it is a literal, verbatim translation or a dynamic equivalent. However, when it comes to interpretation words should be functionally equivalent and culturally sensitive.

Contextualization and Syncretism

There is an important difference between contextualization and syncretism. Contextualization is about finding ways of explaining and exhibiting the gospel that can be understood within a particular cultural context. This is done without compromising the integrity of the message or the messenger. Contextualization recognizes that *what* is expressed can be the same even though *how* it is expressed differs in different times, places and cultures.

Syncretism occurs when the desire to be relevant transcends all other motives. Here both message and messenger become integrated into the prevailing cultural context. Syncretism occurs when Christians adapt, either consciously or unconsciously, to the prevailing worldview. It is the reshaping of Christian beliefs and practices so that they reflect those of the dominant culture. In this process, Christianity loses its distinctiveness. Syncretism often comes from a yearning to make the gospel appear relevant. There is nothing inherently wrong with this desire but it can lead to compromising the truth, and that is a problem. When the church attempts to make its message attractive to outsiders, it must do so without diluting the truth. Some truths are unpopular, but that does not mean that we abandon such biblical truths. The Christian community must be careful not to be swept along by the ebb and flow of cultural currents. If this happens then, the church begins to lose her moorings.

Historical-Grammatical Interpretation

Literal interpretation depends on historical and grammatical exegesis. Exegesis (from the Greek ἐξήγησις from ἐξηγεῖσθαι "to lead out") is an exposition, critical explanation or interpretation of the text. Proper exegesis includes using the context around the passage, comparing it with other parts of the Bible and applying an understanding of the language and customs of the time of the writing. It attempts to understand clearly what the original writer intended to convey. In other words, it is trying to "pull out" of the passage the meaning inherent in it. The opposite of exegesis is *eisegesis*, which is, reading into the text a meaning that does not rightly belong in the passage.

Revealed or Rational?

Is the Bible a revealed or rational text?[1] To say it is revealed is to assert that the Holy Spirit inspired the biblical authors of the texts. Therefore, the words in the Bible convey God's divine revelation to humanity. To say that it is rational is to assert that the original writers of the biblical books used their own creativity ~ it is their own inspiration. In short, some study the Bible, believing that God himself directly inspired its writers. Others approach the Bible as a collection of stories, fables, and myths and see these brought to life through the creativity and imagination of human authors.

We will be approaching the text of Scripture as a work of divine revelation rather than human imagination. One reason for doing this is that the Bible itself clearly states that its writers were inspired and that they were eyewitnesses to what they wrote. So, when we say they were inspired we do not mean it in the sense that Shakespeare was inspired, rather that the inspiration came from God. The Bible teaches that its words came from God to human authors through the power of the Holy Spirit. The apostle Peter said:

> For we did not follow cleverly devised myths when we made known to you the power and coming of our Lord Jesus Christ, but we were eyewitnesses of his majesty. For when he received honor and glory from God the Father, and the voice was borne to him by the Majestic Glory, "This is my beloved Son, with whom I am well pleased," we ourselves heard this very voice borne from heaven, for we were with him on the

---

[1] To say it is revealed does not, of course, make it an irrational text, as God works through the minds and personalities of its authors.

holy mountain. And we have something more sure, the prophetic word, to which you will do well to pay attention as to a lamp shining in a dark place, until the day dawns and the morning star rises in your hearts, knowing this first of all, that no prophecy of Scripture comes from someone's own interpretation. For no prophecy was ever produced by the will of man, but men spoke from God as they were carried along by the Holy Spirit.—2 Peter 1:16-21.

The apostle Paul also said, "All Scripture is breathed out by God and profitable for teaching, for reproof, for correction, and for training in righteousness"—2 Timothy 3:16.

The Principle of Perspicuity

The word *perspicuity* (or *perspicuous*) means "clearly expressed and easily understood." The central message of Scripture is clear. This is especially true in regard to what it says about salvation from sin. However, not all passages of Scripture are equally clear or equally relevant to the message of redemption.

The Christian does not necessarily depend on the expertise of biblical scholars for understanding Scripture. However, one should not ignore the fruits of the technical study of Scripture by biblical scholars.[2]

Scripture is not only inspired by the Holy Spirit, but it is also illuminated by the Holy Spirit who helps the reader (who is indwelt by the Holy Spirit) to understand its meaning. So the Holy Spirit, who inspired the Scriptures, enables the believer to understand how it applies to daily life. Without the aid of the Holy Spirit, the words of the Bible cannot be properly understood. The Holy Spirit acts through the Scripture to produce faith in its message. The Holy Spirit never teaches anyone anything that is contrary to the teaching of Scripture.

Presuppositions

Any pre-understanding that the interpreter brings to Scripture should be in harmony with scriptural teaching. Our presuppositions and assumptions are subject to correction by Scripture. Certain pre-

---

[2] Christian Publishing House suggests that one thing the Christian absolutely should not ignore, if he or she is going to interpret the Scriptures themselves is, the expertise of biblical scholars for understanding how to interpret the Bible, i.e., the rules and principles of biblical interpretation. In other words, every Christian should read a book such as this, which advocates the conservative Grammatical-Historical Method, as opposed to the liberal Historical-Critical Method.

understandings are inconsistent with Scripture, such as Naturalism and Scientism, Evolutionism, Secular Humanism and Relativism. Each of these needs to be defined.

Do we impose our own values and experiences on the text? We naturally use our own experiences and understandings in interpreting any text. We all have certain presuppositions. The way we answer the following questions indicates those presuppositions. Is the supernatural possible? Are miracles possible? Does God speak? There are presuppositions about the nature of the Bible: it is inspired revelation, it is authoritative and true, it is a spiritual document, it is both unified and diverse, and it is understandable. We also accept its canonicity.

Naturalism and Scientism

Naturalism and scientism are very similar. Naturalism is a belief that truth is derived from nature and natural causes, not from revelation. Naturalism is a system of thought that rejects all spiritual and supernatural explanations of the world. It holds that science is the sole basis of what can be known.

Scientism is the use of the scientific method of acquiring knowledge. It applies to traditional sciences or other fields of inquiry such as philosophy, psychology, sociology, etc. Like naturalism, scientism is the belief that science alone can explain phenomena. It is the application of scientific methods to fields unsuitable for it, such as the Bible. The attitude that predominates in scientism is arrogance, which has fostered dogmatism.

Evolutionism

This biological term refers to the theory that all species develop from earlier forms of life. Evolutionism was a common nineteenth-century belief that organisms inherently improve themselves through progressive inherited change over time, and increase in complexity through evolution. The belief went on to include cultural evolution and social evolution.

There are theistic evolutionists, and there are atheistic evolutionists.[3] But the basic premise behind the evolutionary worldview is atheistic. Evolutionism, in its purer form, is the idea that this universe is the result of random cosmic accidents. It asserts that life arose spontaneously via chance chemical processes, and all life-forms are related and share a

---

[3] Theistic evolutionists are those who have managed to reach a compromise between two very distinct world-views: creationism and evolutionism.

common ancestor. As such it is a worldview, which seeks to explain every aspect of this world in which we live. It encompasses a wide variety of topics, from astronomy to chemistry to biology. At its core, it teaches that there were different stages in the evolution of our universe.

Secular Humanism

This is a system of thought that is based on the values that are believed to be best in human beings. It rejects any supernatural authority and affirms a human-based morality. This secular, cultural and intellectual movement of the Renaissance spread throughout Europe. It is a worldview that stresses human values without reference to religion or spirituality. It is a philosophy that is growing in popularity. Secular Humanism rejects faith in seeking solutions to human problems and answers to important human questions, especially questions concerning the origin, purpose, and destiny of mankind.

Relativism

This is the belief that concepts such as right and wrong, goodness and badness, or truth and falsehood are not absolute. It suggests that these change from culture to culture and situation to situation.

Figurative expression

Literal interpretation allows for figurative expressions that employ figures of speech such as metaphor and simile. But figurative interpretation must not add new and foreign meanings which are not found in the text. We must be especially careful about allegorizing the text. In Galatians 4, Paul is speaking of sonship, where he gives an example using Hagar and Sarah, allegorically. Does this mean we can use the Bible as a source for allegory? No, because Paul specifically states that he is allegorizing. He uses Sarah and Hagar as allegorical of slavery to Law under the Old Covenant. This he contrasts to the freedom of grace in the New Covenant.

Context

The context of a passage is of great importance in understanding the meaning. Context should be understood in terms of concentric circles. It must take into account the context of the whole Bible ~ both Old Testament and New Testament. The next circle of interest is the particular book of the Bible ~ what kind of book is it, historical, poetic, legal, wisdom ~ the genre will be critical in determining the meaning of the text. Then one needs to consider the context of the passage and the specific verse(s) within that carefully. A verse out of context can often be taken to mean something completely different from the intended meaning. It is important, therefore, to focus on the context of a verse in its chapter, book and even in its full biblical context.

Submission

The authority of Scripture cannot be separated from the authority of God. Whatever the Bible condemns, God condemns, and whatever the Bible affirms, God affirms. Scripture requires an attitude of faith and submission to its inspiration, veracity, wisdom, efficacy, inerrancy and authority. The reader accepts *what* Scripture says before asking *why*. Certainly, the "why" questions may be asked. When they are investigated with a reverential and humble attitude, the likelihood of arriving at satisfactory answers is greatly enhanced. Thus, reason submits to revelation. In this way, reason becomes a tool to understand truth and not to determine truth. Reason is useful in the investigation, but it is subordinate rather than superior in the process.

Some biblical commands speak universally and are not bound to particular cultures or situations. Other directives are tied to a particular culture and time. Although the distinction between universal and particular mandates is not always easy to make, it is, nevertheless, important to try to distinguish one from the other. Universal mandates cannot be treated as culturally relative. Biblical absolutes are never to be relativized.

Scientific and Historical Truth

The Bible expresses truth in many ways - not always in propositional statements. It contains no errors or factual mistakes ~ that is, the Scriptures as originally given, in the original languages. There may be issues relating to translation, as all translations are acts of interpretation. Since God is the author of all truth, all truths, biblical and extrabiblical, are consistent and cohesive.

What about science, history and the Bible? The assumptions we begin with can affect the way we interpret texts. For example, two texts might appear to contradict each other. If we begin by assuming that this is possible, then we may come to a different conclusion than if we do not have this assumption. Jesus seems to have accepted the Old Testament as authoritative and infallible in all its aspects, even the historical details. The Bible itself makes no distinction between revelatory and non-revelatory

10

data. The Church has historically believed in the infallibility of the Bible. The Bible is God's Word and as such, it has eternal significance. We must not bear false witness about the Word of God.

The Bible is also a human document. It must be understood within the languages, literature, and contexts in which it was written. God's Word to us was first God's Word to someone else. In a sense, we are reading someone else's mail.

The Bible speaks truth when it touches on matters pertaining to nature, history, science, or anything else. It is not, however, a scientific textbook. Therefore, when it speaks of "sunrise" and "sunset" it is merely using observational language in a metaphorical sense ~ in much the same way as we do today. Before it was ever understood that the earth was round the Bible spoke of the earth as a circle, "It is he who sits above the circle of the earth" (Isa. 40:22). Extra-biblical data may have value for clarifying what Scripture teaches and for helping to correct faulty interpretations. However, extra-biblical views never disprove the teaching of Scripture. It is, therefore, false to assert that science disproves the Bible, Christianity or the existence of God. Such assertions are rooted in either ignorance or animosity.

Original Intent

We seek to determine the intent of the author as reflected in the inspired text.[4] However, the human author may not have always been conscious of the full implications of the meaning of his words. For example, with prophecy, meaning may not always be fully "evidenced" until the prophecy is fulfilled. Though God was aware of the fuller implications that would be manifested in the fulfillment, the prophets were not necessarily fully aware.[5]

Progressive Revelation

Progressive revelation is the idea that God has progressively revealed new truth. Charles Hodge says:

> The progressive character of divine revelation is recognized in relation to all the great doctrines of the Bible...What at first is

---

[4] The notion of truth being inherent in the original intended meaning of the author is challenged by postmodern hermeneutics where the individualistic interpretation of the reader has equal, if not superior, validity. This is a complex issue and requires much attention that extends beyond the scope of this book.

[5] This will be dealt with more fully under the heading *Sensus Plenior* (which means fuller sense).

only obscurely intimated is gradually unfolded in subsequent parts of the sacred volume, until the truth is revealed in its fullness.[6]

Literal interpretation recognizes development in the revelation of the person of God, the purposes of God and the administration of these purposes. It is important to recognize the principle of progressive revelation. Failure to grasp this important rule has brought much harm to the church historically. Well-meaning, but misguided, theologians have forced upon the conscience of New Covenant believers practices that were limited to the Old Covenant era. Bernard Ramm says:

> By progressive revelation we mean that the Bible sets forth a movement of God, with the initiative coming from God and not man, in which God brings man up through the theological infancy of the Old Testament to the maturity of the New Testament. This does not mean that there are no mature ideas in the Old Testament nor simple elements in the New Testament. Progressive revelation is the general pattern of revelation...The law was proper as far as it went, but it did not go far enough. It taught a basic morality for the children of Israel, but our Lord elevates the law to a higher level of motivation and spirituality...The morality of the Ten Commandments was a necessary point of beginning in man's ethical, spiritual, and theological development, but the Sermon on the Mount summons believers in God to a much higher level of ethical conduct...This perspective of progressive revelation is very important to the interpreter. He will expect the full revelation of God in the New Testament. He will not force New Testament meanings into the Old, yet he will be able to more fully expound the Old knowing its counterparts in the New. He will adjust his sights to the times, customs, manners, and morals of the people of God at any given state in the Old Testament period of revelation, and he will be aware of partial and elementary nature of the Old Testament revelation. He will take Augustine's words, 'distinguish the times and you will harmonize Scripture,' as a guide so as not to create a contradiction in Scripture by forcing a New Testament standard of morality or doctrine upon an Old Testament passage.[7]

---

[6] Charles Hodge, *Systematic Theology 1*, (Peabody: Hendrickson, 2003), 446.

[7] Bernard Ramm, *Protestant Biblical Interpretation: A Textbook of Hermeneutics*, (3rd edition, Grand Rapids, Mich.: Baker Book House, 1970), 102-104.

Consistency

Hermeneutical consistency must be maintained throughout all biblical passages. Scripture is its own best interpreter. In comparing Scripture with Scripture, the Bible can elucidate a text so that clear passages give light in interpreting unclear passages. However, no passage contradicts another. There may be apparent contradictions, but these can be explained by investigation. Later writers of Scripture never misinterpreted earlier passages of Scripture. Therefore, the New Testament writers never misinterpreted the Old Testament. Thus, New Testament writers never attributed meaning to an Old Testament text, which was not expressed by the author of that text.[8] However, there is sometimes a wide range of *application* for a text. However, the *interpretation* of a biblical text by another biblical writer is always consistent with the meaning of the first text.

Coherence

The inerrancy of Scripture implies that a coherent system of theology is possible, though any human systemization is imperfect. Systemization of theology attempts to fulfill the human intellectual instinct for organization. Understanding the coherence of Scripture protects from heresy and from repeating the doctrinal deviations of history. It aids in interpreting obscure passages of Scripture. It also protects from conflict with logic and demonstrates the harmony of all doctrines.

Preaching

The type of preaching which best conveys the divine revelation is that which faithfully expounds the text of Scripture ~ in other words, biblical preaching. The Bible is a living, dynamic book and it is important that we treat it as such when seeking to understand its contents. Therefore, we must not approach it flippantly, prejudicially or arrogantly. We all have our own biases and assumptions, and so none of us are neutral interpreters of Scripture. But we must aim for objectivity and not allow our preconceived opinions to blind us to the message of the Word. The Bible was not written for the scholar *per se*. But that does not mean we can have a lazy or undisciplined approach to handling it. We should invest the time and effort needed to understand Scripture better. The Bible urges, "Do your best to present yourself to God as one approved, a

---

[8] Although they may not have understood the fuller sense (*Sensus Plenior*) which we will explore later in this work.

worker who has no need to be ashamed, rightly handling the word of truth." (2 Tim. 2:15). Truth is precious; it is worth something, "Buy truth, and do not sell it; buy wisdom, instruction, and understanding" (Prov. 23:23). In the Scriptures, we have an incomparable treasure. Solomon speaks of the value of spiritual wisdom which is contained in Scripture:

> My son, if you receive my words and treasure up my commandments with you, making your ear attentive to wisdom and inclining your heart to understanding; yes, if you call out for insight and raise your voice for understanding, if you seek it like silver and search for it as for hidden treasures, then you will understand the fear of the LORD and find the knowledge of God.—Proverbs. 2:1-5.

For the preacher there must be a desire of the heart ~ crying after knowledge, seeking for an understanding of spiritual things. There should be the kind of ardor and determination that men employ when mining for gold. Our hearts should yearn for a deeper and fuller knowledge of the truth such as men display when searching for hidden treasure. Sadly this is not always the case, as A. W. Pink points out, "People are willing to work and study hard and long to master one of the arts or sciences, but where spiritual and eternal things are concerned it is usually otherwise."[9] Of course, not everybody can be a full-time student of biblical studies or theology, but all believers ought to be diligent in seeking to understand the Bible better.

Advice to Students

An open mind is another prerequisite for the biblical interpreter. We must be aware of our own presuppositions and prejudices. We must fairly evaluate what others, from various theological traditions, have said about the meaning of a text. We need to be careful that we do not limit our avenues for learning by reading only those who support our preconceived opinions. This does not necessarily mean that we have to agree with those in other theological categories, but other interpretive options should be examined before reaching a settled conclusion.

The sound interpreter will accept the inerrancy and authority of Scripture. The Bible is the complete, intelligible and sufficient revelation of God. It is not just for scholars. It can be understood by the simple, "The unfolding of your words gives light; it imparts understanding to the simple." (Ps. 119:130) It is a book intended for the conversion and

---

[9] A.W. Pink; cited in Iain H. Murray, *The Life of Arthur W. Pink*, (Edinburgh: Banner of Truth, 2004), 235.

instruction of people. Of course, Scripture contains passages that are difficult to interpret. At a superficial level, there may appear to be contradictions, which will require diligent study to resolve. The interpreter must retain an attitude of humility bearing in mind that, "For now we see in a mirror dimly." (1 Cor. 13:12). It can be acknowledged that some things in Scripture are hard to understand as Peter said of Paul's letters (2 Pet. 3:16). Nevertheless, the Bible's central message of redemption for lost sinners is clear. As noted earlier, theologians refer to this as the 'perspicuity of Scripture.'

Compare Interpretations/Conclusions with Other Commentators

If the interpreter comes to a novel interpretation of a given passage, it would be wise to compare those conclusions with other commentators. This helps to prevent us from forming incorrect views of the passage or chapter under examination. It thus safeguards the local church from false doctrine. The interpreter should apply this checking principle with scholarly sources in order to obtain reliable information on a passage or subject.

If for example, we are studying a matter that touches on Bible history, we should try to find reliable works in that field.[10] When consulting a commentary, don't limit yourself to just one. Check several commentators before deciding an issue.[11] The checking principle will help us to avoid error and shallowness and will enhance our education in God's Word.

Hermeneutics should not be merely a theoretical exercise. The interpreter must also practically apply what is discovered in the interpretive process. It is not enough to merely *know* ~ we must go on to

---

[10] Such as: Alfred Edersheim, *Old Testament Bible History*; Walter C. Kaiser, *A History of Israel*; F.F. Bruce, *New Testament History* and others.

[11] Some of the best general commentaries on both the Old and New Testaments are, *Baker Exegetical Commentary on the New Testament* (by various authors); *New Testament Commentary* series by William Hendriksen and Simon Kistemaker; *The New International Commentary on the Old Testament & New Testament* (by various authors); *The New American Commentary on the Old Testament & New Testament* (by various authors); *The Expositor's Bible Commentary: Old Testament & New Testament* (by various authors). For commentaries on individual books of the Old Testament see Joel Beeke's list:

http://www.puritanseminary.org/library/Recommended%20OT%20Commentaries.pdf See also the DayOne multiple volume electronic or hardcopy commentaries (commended by John McArthur) http://www.logos.com/product/3984/exploring-the-bible-commentary-collection

do because all knowledge gained from the divine Word brings accountability.—Ezra 7:10; Psalm 119:112; James 1:22.

Why are there so Many Different Interpretations?

Carelessness might account for rash, simplistic, and wrong interpretations. For some people, interpretation is entirely or largely subjective where biblical scholars are ignored. For some scholarship is even despised. This can lead to novel or bizarre interpretations of Scripture. Others lack the gifts or intellectual ability to be mature interpreters of Scripture. The problem is then made worse when such unqualified persons are given a platform whereby they can espouse their distorted views. In this way, wrong opinions of the Bible's meaning are promoted. It is the duty of responsible leadership to keep such people out of the pulpit. We must facilitate opportunities for others to explore, test and develop their gifts and we must be gracious as mistakes will be made.

Another reason for wrong interpretations is an uncritical acceptance of tradition. In such a situation, loyalty is cherished as a virtue.[12] This fosters doctrinaire attitudes that act as a barrier to an impartial investigation. People who are doctrinaire are usually determined to use a specific theory or method and refuse to accept that there might be a better approach. Not every believer has the same level of biblical and spiritual understanding.

Some Christians are not gifted with the necessary insight needed to interpret Scripture. This can be for a variety of reasons, such as hardness of heart. Even the apostles, at one time in their lives, lacked understanding, "...for they did not understand about the loaves, but their hearts were hardened." (Mk. 6:52). In some cases, we may not yet be able to bear such divine truths, "I still have many things to say to you, but you cannot bear them now." (Jn. 16:12). God waits until we mature further.

Lack of Training

Many churches do not offer classes on hermeneutics because pastors are busy. Many churches do not offer classes on hermeneutics because the leadership fails to see the practical relevance of such study. The common assumption seems to be that the study of hermeneutics is for seminary students. It is thought to be too intellectual for the average church

---

[12] Loyalty, like tolerance, is not necessarily virtuous as it depends on what precisely one is loyal to or tolerant of in the first instance. One can be loyal to and tolerant of harmful things.

member. But such thinking is misguided. Bible study is going to be a life-long pursuit for the Christian. For this reason, it is important that they be taught how to interpret properly and apply it. Another problem that I have observed is the training of preachers in homiletics without any foundation in hermeneutics. This is like building on sand ~ foolish!

Interrogate the Text

A basic approach to biblical interpretation will involve interrogating the text. When studying a passage of Scripture, we must ask many questions. Who are the central figures in this passage? Who wrote this book? When was it written? Who is the audience? What is the central message? What is the primary intent of the writer? What are the context and historical setting? What is God trying to teach me? When did this event take place? Where did it take place? Where was the author when he wrote this book or recorded this event? Why did it occur? Why did the writer choose to include this narrative and how does it fit into his particular theme or purpose? How did this happen? How does this narrative relate to other events within the same book? How can I apply this to the circumstances of my life? My own personal favorite question is, "so what?" Of course, I do not ask it irreverently. It is a question, which probes for deeper meaning and searches out the application needed. Ask it seriously of any verse of Scripture and the reward it yields will surprise you. Paul wrote to Timothy, "All Scripture is breathed out by God and profitable for teaching, for reproof, for correction, and for training in righteousness." (2 Tim. 3:16). We, therefore, must always ask of a text ~ how is it profitable in relation to these categories? Context is the fabric of meaning:

> The word context, as the etymology intimates (Latin, *con*, together, and *textus*, woven), denotes something that is woven together, and, applied to a written document, it means the connection of thought supposed to run through every passage which constitutes by itself a whole. By some writers it is called the connection. The immediate context is that which immediately precedes or follows a given word or sentence. The remote context is that which is less closely connected, and may embrace a whole paragraph or section.[13]

When we look at a verse, we must also consider the paragraph where it belongs, the section, book, genre, Testament and the whole Bible. The immediate context for a word or phrase is the verse where it appears. The wider context is the chapter. Chapters divisions are generally

---

[13] Milton S. Terry, *Biblical Hermeneutics: a Treatise on the Interpretation of the Old and New Testaments*, (Grand Rapids, Michigan: Zondervan, 1974), 210.

helpful segments but they are artificially imposed, and we should be aware of this. The wider context should include the whole book. The widest context is the entire Bible. One must try to understand how the word, phrase or sentence is used elsewhere in Scripture.

CHAPTER 2 Why Is Hermeneutics Important

Let's just remind ourselves of the meaning of hermeneutics. The word "hermeneutics" is derived from the Greek word ἑρμηνεύω (hermeneuō) which means to translate or interpret. It is derived from Greek mythology which gives an account of Hermes, the Greek god who brought the messages of the gods to humans, which he also interpreted. Thus, the word hermeneuō came to refer to bringing someone to an understanding of something. Biblical hermeneutics is the science and art of interpreting the Bible. By means of various principles, it seeks to discover the precise meaning of the original authors of Scripture.

The Bible contains several passages that suggest the importance of proper interpretation in order to arrive at a true understanding. In a passage where Ezra read the Law from a wooden platform constructed for that purpose, it is stated, "They read from the book, from the Law of God, clearly, and they gave the sense, so that the people understood the reading."—Nehemiah 8:8.

On the road to Emmaus Jesus said:

"O foolish ones, and slow of heart to believe all that the prophets have spoken! Was it not necessary that the Christ should suffer these things and enter into his glory?" And beginning with Moses and all the Prophets, he interpreted to them in all the Scriptures the things concerning himself.—Luke 24:25-27.

When Paul and Silas were in Berea they encountered some curious unbelievers: It is recorded of these Bereans, "...they received the word with all eagerness, examining the Scriptures daily to see if these things were so."—Acts 17:11.

Philip asked the Ethiopian eunuch, who was reading Isaiah 53, "Do you understand what you are reading?" (Acts 8:30). The eunuch answered, "How can I, unless someone guides me?" (v.31). The eunuch did not understand the messianic significance of this passage until Philip explained the gospel from this text.—Acts 8:27-35.

Peter says, "Paul also wrote to you according to the wisdom given him, as he does in all his letters when he speaks in them of these matters. There are some things in them that are hard to understand, which the ignorant and unstable twist to their own destruction, as they do the other Scriptures." (2 Pet. 3:16) Interestingly Peter is referring to the writings of Paul as "Scripture."

As a theological discipline, hermeneutics seeks a correct interpretation of the Bible. To this end, it seeks to formulate principles of interpretation. These principles or rules are like a rulebook for a game. The game is meaningless without the rules, "Hermeneutics...is like a cookbook and exegesis is the preparing and baking of the cake and exposition is serving the cake"[14] How important is hermeneutics compared to other theological disciplines? Its importance is immense since a proper understanding of Scripture is the basis of a sound theology. A trustworthy interpretation of Scripture, therefore, is critical for a proper understanding of the Christian faith.

A sound and trustworthy interpretation of the Scripture...is the root and basis of all revealed theology. Without it Systematic Theology, or Dogmatics, could not be legitimately constructed, and would, in fact, be essentially impossible. For the doctrines of revelation can only be learned from a correct understanding of the oracles of God.[15]

The study of hermeneutics is an important and relevant subject for every Christian. The world of the Bible is widely separated in its culture and customs from our world today. Therefore, there is the need to bridge that gap. There is a wide range of literary genres found in the Bible (e.g., poetry, prophecy, parables and so on) and there are ancient figures of speech, and this makes hermeneutics necessary for biblical interpretation. We all bring our own theological baggage to the task of interpretation, but hermeneutics is meant to be impartial and objective not biased and subjective. This is the problem with some approaches to interpretation, which are agenda-driven ~ such as, Liberation, Feminist and Black theologies. These approaches are not independent, and many of its scholars are propagandists. Therefore, hermeneutics is important for constructing theological understandings. One author puts it like this:

> Exegesis is prior to any system of theology...We can only know the truth of God by a correct exegesis of Scripture...Great mischief has been done in the church when the system of theology or its framework has been derived extra-biblically...If the grounds of Christian theology is the revelation of God, then theology must be grounded in revelation and not in philosophy. The historic Protestant position is to ground theology in biblical exegesis. A theological system is to be built up exegetically brick by brick. Hence, the theology is no better than the exegesis that underlies it. The task of the systematic

---

[14] Roy B. Zuck, *Basic Bible Interpretation*, (David C. Cook, 1991), 22.

[15] Milton S. Terry, *Biblical Hermeneutics: a Treatise on the Interpretation of the Old and New Testaments*, (Grand Rapids, Michigan: Zondervan, 1974), 21-22.

theologian is to commence with these bricks ascertained through exegesis, and build the temple of his theological system.[16]

Careful hermeneutics will keep people from drifting into heresy or falling prey to a religious cult. As James Sire has noted:

If traditional Christianity affirms the Bible as its sole authority, *Sola Scriptura*, as the Reformers said, how can these very different religious movements [i.e., Jehovah's Witnesses, Mormons, Christian Science] claim Scripture for their own? The obvious answer is the right one, I believe. They can only do so by violating the principles of sound literary interpretation.[17]

Therefore, a sound hermeneutic is critical, especially a clear understanding of the differences which exist between the Old and New Covenants. This will help us to avoid making wrong deductions. Making wrong deductions from the Old Testament is a common mistake. Throughout church history, it has led to all sorts of abuses and atrocities:

Because Scripture has not been properly interpreted the following has been urged as the voice of God: in that the patriarchs practiced polygamy we may practice it; in that the Old Testament sanctioned the divine right of the king of Israel, we may sanction the divine right of kings everywhere; because the Old Testament sanctioned the death of witches, we too may put them to death; because the Old Testament declared that some plagues were from God, we may not use methods of sanitation, for that would be thwarting the purposes of God; because the Old Testament forbade usury in the agrarian commonwealth of Israel we may not employ it in our economic system; because the Scriptures make certain remarks about the suffering of women in childbirth we may not approve any method of easing the pain; because tithing was a law (*de jure*) in Israel, it is a law to the Church...A sound hermeneutics would have prevented all of this. It would prevent an uncritical and unrealistic application of the Old Testament to Christian morality. It would prevent an expositor from using some mere phrase as an eternal principle of morality. It would prevent the effort of trying to force some binding principle upon contemporary life from an obscure Old Testament incident. It would prevent the justification of ritualism and priestcraft from

---

[16] Bernard Ramm, *Protestant Biblical Interpretation: A Textbook of Hermeneutics,* (Baker Academic, 1980), 168-169.

[17] James Sire, *Scripture Twisting: 20 Ways the Cults Misread the Bible,* (IVP, 1980), 12.

an improper extension of the Tabernacle worship and sacrificial system. The result of an erratic hermeneutics is that the Bible has been made the source of confusion rather than light.[18]

```
See Appendix 4: Tithing ~ A Case Study
```

Three Categories of Law

The Mosaic Law falls into three categories, moral, ceremonial and judicial. These distinctions are important ~ especially when it comes to issues like capital punishment. The prohibition against murder comes under the absolute moral law. However, the death penalty was prescribed under the judicial aspect of the law and need not necessarily be the only punishment for murder. Because the penalty is a judicial matter, it is up to the state to decide. Therefore, Christians who say the Bible requires the death penalty for murderers are wrong. Likewise Christians who say it is wrong for the state to impose the death penalty, because killing is prohibited in Scripture are also wrong. It comes down to proper hermeneutics.

The ceremonial law, with its many offerings and sacrifices, was fulfilled in Christ. Jesus was the fulfillment of all that was typified by those ordinances. Therefore, they are no longer necessary or relevant. The judicial law set out the manner in which Israel's society was to be governed and regulated. This also passed away in A. D. 70 when the Jewish nation was scattered and therefore ceased to exist. The moral law (the Ten Commandments) is the abiding law of God for all time and did not pass with the coming of Christ.[19] Usually, reference to the law of God in the New Testament refers to the *Ten Commandments*. There is never a hint given that this has been repealed. These commands are the transcript of holiness and as such, they are the divine standard. They were written first upon the heart of Adam before they were inscribed on tablets of stone at Sinai. This moral law is binding upon all men for all time. Man is responsible and accountable to the standard. It is impossible to keep. Jesus is the only person who has ever kept the law in its entirety. It is a serious matter for any person to dismiss the law of God as irrelevant. This applies to people both inside and outside the church. The believer is no longer under the law in terms of justification ~ that is to say nobody can be justified by keeping the law. The absolute moral law of God has never

---

[18] Bernard Ramm, *Protestant Biblical Interpretation*, 2-3.
[19] Salvation is by grace alone, through faith alone, in Christ alone. The law convicts of sin and is a signpost to Christ, who paid the penalty for the sins

22

been revoked. We are expected to conform to its requirements for holy living.

Contemporary Issues

Proper hermeneutics is important for interpreting Scripture in relation to contemporary social and spiritual issues. It would prevent an expositor from using some mere phrase as an eternal principle of morality ~ for example, the Jehovah's Witnesses attitude to blood transfusions. It would prevent some binding principle being forced upon contemporary life from an obscure Old Testament incident. The result of bad hermeneutics is that the Bible has been made the source of confusion rather than light. The goal of hermeneutics is that we might be better interpreters of Scripture and thereby, kept from doctrinal error and many other abuses that arise from a mishandling of Scripture. Hermeneutics is important for spiritual development because correct application of biblical truth depends on correct interpretation. It is relevant in determining what the Christian believes and how the Christian lives.

CHAPTER 3 Necessary Qualifications for the Biblical Interpreter

Spiritual truth can only be fully comprehended when the Holy Spirit illuminates a person's mind. Spiritual regeneration is necessary in order to understand properly and apply Scripture. The Bible is a sacred book and is discerned best by those who are spiritually regenerated ~ i.e. born again. The apostle Paul said:

> The natural person does not accept the things of the Spirit of God, for they are folly to him, and he is not able to understand them because they are spiritually discerned. The spiritual person judges all things, but is himself to be judged by no one. "For who has understood the mind of the Lord so as to instruct him?" But we have the mind of Christ—1 Corinthians 2:14-16.

Robert H. Stein in, *A Basic Guide to Interpreting the Bible*, speaking of 2 Corinthians 2:14, writes, "This is interpreted as meaning that, apart from the Spirit, a person cannot "understand" the meaning of biblical texts. Without the Spirit these texts are simply foolish riddles. Yet before we assume that Paul, and the English translators of Paul, are using the term "understand" in the exact sense in which we defined the term in chapter 2, we must look more closely at this verse."

Stein continues, "What does Paul mean when he says that apart from the Spirit these things are 'foolishness'? Does he mean that a person without the Spirit will not be able to come to a correct mental grasp of what the biblical text means? Is Paul saying that apart from the Spirit the biblical teachings are incomprehensible?"

Stein goes on to say that the "meaning of the term 'foolishness' is best understood by observing how Paul uses it elsewhere. In 1 Corinthians 3:19 the term is used as follows: 'For the wisdom of this world is foolishness in God's sight.' Here, it should be noted, something is foolish to God! Clearly Paul does not mean that God cannot arrive at a correct mental grasp of what this world calls wisdom! God is omniscient; he understands everything. God, of course, understands what this world calls wisdom. He rejects it, however, as foolishness. The term 'foolishness' in 1 Corinthians 3:19 refers not to what we have called 'understanding' but rather to 'significance.' God understands perfectly well what this world calls wisdom, but he critiques it. He evaluates it. He condemns it as foolishness. In 1 Corinthians 1:20 the verbal form of this word is used, and Paul states similarly, 'Has not God made foolish the wisdom of the world?' Here (1:20), in the chapter before 1 Corinthians 2:14, as well as in the chapter following (3:19), Paul uses the expression 'foolish' to refer to the significance God attributes to something (this world's wisdom)."

Stein then asks, "Should this same meaning be attributed to the term in 1 Corinthians 2:14? It would appear so, for what Paul is saying is not that unbelievers cannot arrive at a correct mental grasp of the things of the Spirit. They can and do, but they attribute to this understanding of the author's meaning a negative significance. They reject it as 'foolishness.' Thus, in the first three chapters of 1 Corinthians we have the following parallel. The unbelieving world can understand the things of the Spirit, what the biblical text means, but it rejects what it understands as foolishness. Similarly, God understands the wisdom of this world, but rejects it as foolishness. In both instances there is a correct mental grasp of what is meant (understanding) followed by a rejection of its value (significance)."

Finally, Stein concludes, "In a similar way it would appear that the terms for 'understand' in 1 Corinthians 2:12 and 14 are best understood as meaning something different than acquiring a correct mental grasp of meaning. It refers rather to embracing as true these biblical truths. It is probably best to see the terms 'does not accept,' 'foolishness,' and "cannot understand" as referring to various ways in which the unbeliever critiques the divine revelation. This critique (significance) is based on an understanding of that message. The understanding of the text is rejected in several different ways: (1) it is not accepted, not received eagerly or welcomed, because it is opposed to human wisdom (cf. 1 Cor. 1:18–25); (2) it is judged as foolishness because it conflicts with their sense of truth; and (3) it is not believed as being true because only the Spirit can convince us of the truth of the gospel message. It would appear that whereas 1 Corinthians 2:14 refers to the work of the Spirit in 'conviction' or 'significance,' it does not deny but rather assumes that an unbeliever can 'understand' the gospel message."— (Stein 1994, 66-7)

Unbelieving scholars might be able to contribute to a better understanding of contextual (historical and cultural) issues but the unregenerate mind is at enmity with God, "For the mind that is set on the flesh is hostile to God, for it does not submit to God's law; indeed, it cannot. Those who are in the flesh cannot please God." (Rom. 8:7-8). So Scripture itself teaches that the unregenerate mind cannot understand the true significance of divine revelation. Such an interpreter cannot be trusted to decipher the spiritual meaning. Such interpreters can have an intellectual comprehension but will not have a spiritual apprehension of truth. In other words, they simply do not have the power or ability to grasp the importance, significance, or meaning of something in its fullest spiritual sense.

Competent to Comment

I was listening to a radio interview in Ireland with Vincent Browne, a TV and radio chat show host admired by the public and feared by politicians. Vincent Browne is an Irish print and broadcast journalist and a non-practicing barrister. *The Guardian* has described him as an "acerbic host...Ireland's Jeremy Paxman."[20]

On this occasion, he was the interviewee rather than the interviewer. He is an intelligent man without a doubt and in many ways, I admire him. However, in the course of the interview, he said, "If you ever doubt your atheism, read the Bible," ~ meaning it will affirm your atheism. He then alluded to Judges, chapter 19. This is a disturbing passage of Scripture about a Levite and his concubine that led to the battle of Gibeah episode as recorded in the book of Judges.

The battle was triggered by an incident in which the concubine of a man from the Tribe of Levi was raped, by members of the Tribe of Benjamin, and later died. The Levite had offered his concubine to the mob in his place. In the morning, he found the concubine unresponsive on the doorstep ~ probably dead. He later cut her dead body into twelve pieces and sent the pieces throughout all the territories of the Israelite tribes.

The outraged tribes of Israel sought justice and demanded that the perpetrators be delivered for judgment. The Benjamites refused, so the tribes then sought vengeance, and in the subsequent war, the members of the Tribe of Benjamin were systematically killed, including women and children; when the tribe of Benjamin was almost exterminated it was decided that the tribe should be allowed to survive, and all the men from another town, Jabesh Gilead, who had refused to take part in the punishment of the Tribe of Benjamin, were killed, so that their daughters could be wed to the surviving men of Benjamin. The first king of Israel, Saul, descended from these men. Due to this war, the Tribe of Benjamin was subsequently referred to as the smallest of all the tribes.

How are we to understand this shocking and disturbing passage of Scripture? For Vincent Browne, it is an affirmation of atheism. But his comments bring to mind the saying, "fools rush in where angels fear to tread." How can such an intellectual be so devoid of understanding?

---

[20] Michael White, "An Irish election in a time of staggering debt and quiet rage," *The Guardian*. 14 February 2011. Jeremy Paxman is an English broadcaster, journalist and author. He has worked for the BBC since 1972 and is known for his forthright and abrasive interviewing style, particularly when interrogating politicians.

This story parallels one of Lot's experiences with the two angels in Sodom and bears witness to the Lord's abhorrence of illicit and violent (particularly non-consensual) sexual behavior whether homosexual or heterosexual. It also underscores what soon happens in a society that abandons God. This incident took place within one generation after the Israelites had conquered the land, and since the fathers didn't teach their children what the Lord had done for them, the nation quickly sank into one of the most morally and spiritually corrupt times in its history.

Relative Morality

A recurring theme in Judges is that "In those days Israel had no King, and everyone did what was right in his own sight." The real lesson of Judges is the moral disaster that ensues when people abandon God, and everyone decides for himself what is right. It is an appalling picture of lawlessness and moral depravity. The incident is recorded (not affirmed) rather than airbrushed out of the history of Israel so that people might understand the depravity of man.

Therefore, Vincent Browne's interpretation of that biblical incident is blissfully unaware of the principles of biblical interpretation, proving that even the wisest of men are not competent to interpret Scripture without the aid of the Holy Spirit. His opinions about the Bible are not just silly; they are absurd and dangerous. It is yet another example of aggressive atheism in the media. Even a basic course in hermeneutics would help him see the passage in context and understand the intended meaning of the original author.

Spiritual Leaders

Even spiritual leaders can be ignorant of the significance of Scripture. For example, in the *Gospel of Matthew* it is recorded that King Herod inquired of the chief priests and scribes as to where the Messiah was to be born (Mt. 2:3-4). They were able to point him correctly to the prediction of Micah 5:2, which foretold that the King of Israel would be born in Bethlehem. Yet they were blinded and apathetic to the possibility that the Messiah might have now appeared. This attitude contrasts with the Magi who had claimed to see the guiding star in the east (v.2) and were obviously interested.

Jesus accused the Sadducees of ignorance, "You are wrong, because you know neither the Scriptures nor the power of God." (Mt. 22:23-29) Throughout the gospels, we find Jesus accusing very learned men (who were experts in Judaic Law) of ignorance concerning the Scriptures. Sadly, there are many religious leaders today of whom it may be said, "You are wrong, because you know neither the Scriptures nor the power of God."

Later, the Pharisees were also silenced when they were unable to answer Jesus' question about the Christological meaning of Psalm 110:1 in a passage about the identity of Jesus:

> And as Jesus taught in the temple, he said, "How can the scribes say that the Christ is the son of David? David himself, in the Holy Spirit, declared, "'The Lord said to my Lord, Sit at my right hand, until I put your enemies under your feet.' David himself calls him Lord. So how is he his son?" And the great throng heard him gladly.—Mark 12:35-37.

Jesus is in the temple teaching the Word of God. The Pharisees, Sadducees, and Scribes are still looking for a way to discredit Jesus in the eyes of the people and the Roman authorities. These groups questioned Jesus. Their questions were designed to trap him and undermine his authority. However, Jesus answered well and outsmarted these deceitful and dangerous people. He gave his enemies no legitimate cause to bring a charge against him.

Going on the Offensive

All along Jesus had been on the defensive as he responded to their questions. Now Jesus goes on the offensive. He takes the initiative. The question he asked the scribes and Pharisees goes to the heart of what they believe about the identity of Christ. This is a relevant and important question today. Jesus countered every attack his enemies used against him. He answered their question about paying tribute money to Caesar (Mk. 12:13-17); the resurrection and the nature of life in heaven (Mk. 12:18-27) and which commandment in the Law was the greatest (Mk. 12:28-34). Each time Jesus was asked questions that were designed to make him look foolish in the eyes of the people. Every question they asked was an attempt to prove his ignorance of the Old Testament Scriptures. They tried their best to unmask Jesus and prove that he was an imposter.

Now Jesus asks in what sense the Messiah was the Son of David. He did not receive an answer. It is not clear if Jesus waited for an answer but it is likely that there was some silent pause. Whether that silence was the result of ignorance, fear, inability or unwillingness to answer is not certain. The fact remains that Jesus did not receive an answer. So the Lord answered his own question and in doing so confirms the messianic usage of this psalm.

David called the Messiah "My Lord." How could he be both David's son and David's Lord? The Messiah, though David's descendant is also the Son of God and therefore, senior in rank and authority. I can imagine the crowds enjoying Jesus outsmarting the Scribes. Not all Scribes were frauds, but many abused their position and influence. They liked being addressed by honorific titles (rabbi and master). In the synagogue, they sat in a prominent position on a bench in front of the Ark of the Covenant that contained the sacred scrolls. Jesus condemned them for seeking honor for themselves instead of glorifying God, whom they professed to serve. He also criticized them for their long prayers and hypocrisy.

Jesus had answered all their questions. (Mk. 12:34) Now he has a question for them. That question was meant to focus their attention on the person of the Messiah. Jesus asked them, "How can the scribes say that the Christ is the son of David?" Every Jew believed that the Messiah would be a physical descendant of King David. They believed that the Christ would be a great political and military leader who would deliver Israel from those who oppressed them. They believed that the Christ would be a great king in this temporal world. The Jews were looking for a human being. Jesus is about to show them that the Messiah will be human, but he will also be divine. He confronts them about their beliefs concerning the nature and identity of the Messiah.

Grasping the Truth

Many people in the Western world are like the scribes and the Pharisees. They know the Bible stories about Jesus. Some even love the image of that baby in his manger. They have heard about Jesus feeding multitudes, healing the sick, preaching sermons, raising the dead and walking on water. They know the story of the cross and the resurrection. But many people today cannot grasp the truth that Jesus Christ is more than a baby in a manger or a man who was crucified. They cannot seem to grasp the truth that he is God in human flesh.

People will go so far, but they often will not go far enough. Some people are "not far from the kingdom of God." They are on the threshold of belief. However, being "not far" means you are lost. It is like being nearly saved. I would prefer to be nearly drowned than nearly saved, wouldn't you? "Not far" is not where a person needs to remain. A person should not remain undecided about the identity of Jesus. A person should not remain on the threshold of faith. We need to come to Jesus Christ and call on him for salvation. He is the door that leads to eternal life (Jn. 10:9). With him, you are saved; without him you are lost (1 Jn. 5:12). This is an unpalatable truth. Many are willing to believe Jesus was a great teacher, a prophet, a good man, but stop short of believing in his divine identity. They will not accept his unique and universal claims. This has serious consequences.

Confounding the Wise

As Jesus confronts these men, he asks them about Psalm 110:1. That verse was acknowledged by all Jews to be a reference to the coming Messiah. Jesus points out that a careful reading of that verse reveals the truth that the Messiah will be more than a man. The first "Lord," in Psalm 110:1, is the Hebrew word, *Yahweh*. The second "Lord" in that verse is the Hebrew word *Adonai*. The idea in this verse is that "the Lord (*Yahweh*) said to my (David's) Lord (*Adonai*)..." In other words, David addresses the Messiah as his Lord. The implication is clear. The Messiah is to be a man, but he will be more than a man. He is to be God as well. Jesus is declaring the deity of the Messiah.

David was speaking under the inspiration of the Holy Spirit: "The LORD says to my Lord: 'Sit at my right hand until I make your enemies your footstool.'" He placed the Messiah in a position of authority that was co-equal with Almighty God. The word "sit" in that verse speaks of a continuous sitting. The Messiah has a place of equal exaltation with God (Phil. 2:9-11). The Messiah must be God because he will be in a position of absolute equality with God in honor, power and glory. The implication of this can be seen in what Jesus said next, "David himself calls him Lord. So how is he his son?" In that society, a father would never call his son "Lord." A father never rendered that kind of honor to a child. Children were considered to be subordinate and never superior to their fathers. Yet, David looks at this one who is to be his son and David calls him Lord. This is a declaration that the Messiah is to be more than a man. He is to be God and man.

When the Jewish religious leaders heard this, they were dumbfounded. They had no answer. This allegedly unlearned carpenter had put them to shame in the very area where they were supposed to be the experts. Jesus had interpreted the Scriptures in an accurate, clear way that they could not refute.

The Real Jesus

They did not believe Jesus was the Messiah. But Jesus had proven his identity time and again. His place of birth fulfilled prophecy. His triumphal entry into Jerusalem fulfilled prophecy (in detail) concerning the Messiah. He arrived in the precise way that the prophet Zechariah said the Messiah would come (Zech. 9:9). His words, works, and wisdom proved his identity. He fulfilled every Old Testament prophecy that predicted what the Messiah would do when he came (Isa. 29:18-19; 35:3-6; 61:1-2). He healed the sick, raised the dead, forgave sins, walked on water, calmed a storm and cast out demons. The Messiah was to be the Son of David.—2 Samuel 7:8-16; Isaiah 9:7; Jeremiah 23:5.

According to the genealogies (Matthew and Luke), Jesus was a direct descendant of David. On many occasions, Jesus was called "Son of David." Jesus was a man. He had a human mother (Lk. 1:31; Gal. 4:4). He had a human body, soul, and spirit (Mt. 26:12; 38; Lk. 23:46). The soul is the essence of the human being; it is who we are. The spirit is that aspect of the human being that connects with God. He had flesh and blood (Heb. 2:14). He grew (Lk. 2:52). He asked questions (Lk. 2:46) and increased in wisdom (Lk. 2:52). He prayed (Mk. 1:35; Lk. 11:1). He was tempted (Mt. 4:1; Heb. 2:18; 4:15). He learned obedience (Heb. 5:8). He hungered (Mt. 4:2; 21:18) and thirsted (Jn. 4:7; 19:28). He was weary (Jn. 4:6) and slept (Mt. 8:24; Mk. 10:21). He had compassion (Mt. 9:36). He was angered and grieved (Mk. 3:5). He wept (Jn. 11:35; Lk. 19:41). He was troubled (Jn. 11:33; 12:27; 13:21; Mk. 14:33-34). He suffered (1 Pet. 4:1) and bled (Jn. 19:34). He died (Mt. 27:50; 1 Cor. 15:3) and was buried.—Matthew 27:59-60.

Jesus was also God. When Jesus came into this world he was God born as a male child. That is the teaching of the Word of God (Jn. 1:1; 14; Phil. 2:5-8). The evidence from his life proves this too. He is omnipresent (Mt. 18:20; 28:20). He is omnipotent (Mt. 28:18; Heb. 1:3). He has authority over disease (Mt. 4:23). He has authority over Satan (Mt. 4:10; Jn. 12:31; Heb. 2:14). He has authority over demons (Mt. 8:16). He has authority over men (Jn. 17:2). He has authority over nature (Mt. 8:26-27). He has authority over sin (1 Jn. 3:5). He has authority over the Sabbath (Mt. 12:8). He has authority over death itself: physical death (Jn. 5:28-29) and spiritual death.—John 5:24; Hebrews 2:15.

He knew the history of the Samaritan woman (Jn. 4:29). He knew what the scribes and Pharisees were thinking (Mt. 9:3-4; 12:25). He knew the true nature of Judas (Jn. 6:70; 13:11). Jesus receives worship: from the angels (Heb. 1:6); from the magi (Mt. 2:11); from the apostle Thomas (Jn. 20:28). He forgives sin (Mk. 2:5; Jn. 8:24). He possesses all authority (Mt. 7:29). This was reflected in his teaching, which was more than a confident style. He is the source of life itself (Jn. 1:4; Jn. 5:26). He is the creator of all things (Jn. 1:3; Col. 1:16; Heb. 1:2). He is the preserver of all things (Col. 1:17; Heb. 1:3). He receives our prayers (Acts 7:59). He is the final judge (Mt. 25:31-32; Jn. 5:22, 27; Acts 17:31). He is both the Lord of Glory and King of kings.—Revelation 19:16.

Jesus proved his identity. Yet many Jews refused to accept him. They refused to acknowledge him as their Messiah. (Jn. 1:11, Lk. 19:14; Jn.

19:15) Israel had all the evidence they needed to believe in Jesus. They had all the Old Testament prophecies that he had fulfilled to the letter. They had the proof in the temple records that Jesus was a descendant of King David. They had the evidence of changed lives all around them. There were people who had been sick that were now well. Blind people could see. Deaf people could hear. There were demoniacs who had been delivered. In addition, most amazing of all, there were a few people walking around that used to be dead! Many Jews ignored that evidence.

We have far more evidence than they had. We have a completed Bible (Old and New Testaments). We can see where prophecies were made and fulfilled. We too can look around us and we can see lives changed by the amazing grace of God. We have every reason to believe that he is who he claims to be. Believe it and be bold about it in bearing true testimony to him. Luke speaks of; "the church of God, which he obtained with his own blood." (Acts 20:28)[21] This verse nails his deity to the cross.

What does all of this mean? It simply means that even intelligent people and religious leaders may not necessarily be competent to interpret Scripture in an appropriate manner. However, those who are in right relationship with God (not the same as being religious) will know the aid of the Holy Spirit in interpreting Scripture.

What is Necessary for Proper Interpretation?

How can we understand God's message and avoid misunderstandings about the Bible? As already noted, we must have a proper understanding of the genre. A good translation is important. Asking the right questions is important. There are factors that depend on the individual. Is there a genuine desire to understand the text? There must be faith. Only those who believe and trust in God can truly understand what God is saying in Scripture. Does the reader have a heart that is willing to obey the text?

Prayer and dependence on the Holy Spirit are vital in the process of hermeneutics. Prayer places us in the position where we can hear the Spirit and understand the text. The same Holy Spirit, who provided the inspiration to the writers of Scripture, also provides illumination to the interpreters of Scripture. Interpretation requires the illumination of the

---

[21] As to this particular rendering in Acts 20:28, the Revised Standard Version, and the Lexham English Bible, is the preferred translation for Christian Publishing House, "the church of God which he obtained with the blood of his own Son." See the article, *Acts 20:28—A Worthy Translation is Faithful*: http://www.uasvbible.org/translation-acts-20-28

Spirit. Neither methodology nor the Spirit operates in isolation from the other. The Spirit's work of illumination does not grant new revelation.

Spiritual Commitment

There must be a spiritual commitment on the part of the interpreter. (1 Cor.2:6-14; Eph.4:17-24; Rom.8) To merely understand what the text says can be done by anyone who has been trained. Anyone can lay out the various options of interpretation. However, those who are committed can only exercise obedience to the text.

Common Sense

Much of the Bible is understandable even without extensive knowledge of the literature and context in which it was written. We interpret with other Christians. Theology should not be done on one's own. There should be an understanding of the story line of the Bible, not just dipping in here and there. Thus, systematic, regular reading should be a central part of our lives (devotional and scholarly). Pastors and preachers should not just use the Word as a resource. They should not just trawl for sermons. They must also feed their souls and find a word in season. We must understand that the Bible points to salvation through the person of Jesus.

Everyone is an exegete, but not everyone is a good one! The proper interpretation of a text begins with the exegesis of a text. There are a couple of lines from a hymn that goes, "Wonderful things in the Bible I see, this is the dearest, that Jesus loves me." But some people could sing, "Wonderful things in the Bible I see, most of them put there by you and me."

CHAPTER 4 A Literal-Historical-Grammatical Approach

The historical-grammatical method of interpretation is necessary if one is going to interpret the Bible rightly. This means that the interpreter must be sensitive to the historical context and setting of the passage under examination. It also means that the interpreter must be sensitive to its grammar or word usage. Another term frequently used by theologians is "literal interpretation." It is commonly used in its dictionary sense, "...the natural or usual construction and implication of a writing or expression; following the ordinary and apparent sense of words; not allegorical or metaphorical."[22]

Although there are elements of allegory in Scripture, the Bible is not an allegorical book. An allegorical work is one in which the characters and events are understood as representing other things. An allegorical work symbolically expresses a deeper, often spiritual, moral, or political meaning ~ for example, George Orwell's *Animal Farm*, which is a political allegory.

A metaphor is a figure of speech that describes a subject by asserting that it is, on some point of comparison, the same as another otherwise unrelated object. It is not meant to be taken literally. A metaphor by means of a vivid comparison expresses something about him, her, or it. A metaphor is making a comparison without the use of the word "like" or "as." For example, saying that somebody is a snake. A simile is a figure of speech that draws a comparison between two different things, especially a phrase containing the word "like" or "as." For example, "as white as a sheet."

Literal interpretation does not mean a kind of wooden literalism. It is about the usual, customary, or normal sense of words. Literal interpretation recognizes nuances, metaphors, similes hyperbole, symbolism, plays on words, or the various figures of speech which the biblical writers frequently used. Hyperbole is a deliberate and obvious exaggeration used for effect, e.g., "I could eat a million of these." Hyperbole is used in Scripture, and it is important to recognize it. We will deal with these figures of speech in more detail later.

Normally when a person says something or writes something he does not intend that a diversity of meanings should be attached to what he says or writes. Usually, his listeners or readers understand the obvious sense. The late Old Testament scholar, Oswald T. Allis, has written, "No

---

[22] *Webster's New International Dictionary.*

literalist, however, thoroughgoing, takes everything in the Bible literally. Nor do those who lean to a more figurative method of interpretation insist that everything is figurative. Both principles have their proper place and their necessary limitations."[23] Therefore, it is important to qualify the meaning of "literal interpretation" in order to avoid misunderstanding what is intended by the phrase.

The advantage of the literal or historical-grammatical interpretation is that it is the method usually practiced in the interpretation of literature. It is the usual method used for ancient or modern, sacred or secular texts.

The postmodern approach is different because it does not seek authorial intent. For the postmodern interpreter, it is the individual reader or community, which gives meaning to the text. This has spawned a whole new area of hermeneutics.[24]

The literal or historical-grammatical method controls the exegete from falling prey to common abuses of Scripture. That is, common abuses such as mystical and allegorical forms of interpretation. We must permit clear or plain passages of Scripture to explain those which are more obscure or difficult. Thus, Scripture interprets Scripture. This requires a careful comparison of one verse with another. This ensures a legitimate parallel in thought or doctrine and not merely a verbal one. Thus, we may clarify a passage which was previously shrouded in mystery. The Protestant Reformers spoke of this principle as the *analogia Scriptura* (analogy of Scripture). This means that since the Bible does not contradict itself, we must look to other passages of the Word to help illumine those which are less clear. As J. I. Packer has stated:

> The Bible appears like a symphony orchestra, with the Holy Ghost as its Toscanini; each instrumentalist has been brought willingly, spontaneously, creatively, to play his notes just as the great conductor desired, though none of them could ever hear the music as a whole...The point of each part only becomes fully clear when seen in relation to all the rest.[25]

We must be always aware of the historical background because the Bible was written within human history. The interpreter must seek to be informed about the historical events and culture in which the passage was conceived. Many Bible study tools and resources enable biblical students to bridge the historical and cultural gap between the ancient biblical

---

[23] Oswald T. Allis, *Prophecy and the Church*, (Wipf & Stock, 2001), 17.

[24] This would be a separate study.

[25] J. I. Packer, *God Has Spoken: Revelation and the Bible*, (Baker Academic, 1994), 74.

world and our world in the twenty-first century. As H. H. Rowley points out:

> A religion which is thus rooted and grounded in history cannot ignore history. Hence a historical understanding of the Bible is not a superfluity which can be dispensed with in biblical interpretation, leaving a body of ideas and principles divorced from the process out of which they were born.[26]

Distinguish Between What the Bible Records and What it Approves

The inexperienced Bible reader may make the mistake of assuming that because Scripture records the actions of a character that God endorses such action. The Bible is a record of redemptive history, which records a variety of deeds on the part of humans (both good and bad). Every instance noted within its pages is not morally evaluated in explicit terms. We may have to consider other hermeneutical factors in order to arrive at a conclusion concerning the morality of the incident set forth.

For example, 1 Samuel 25 records an incident when David was prepared to slaughter Nabal and his entire household (v.17). This was because of Nabal's lack of hospitality and disrespectful words toward David and his servants (vs. 3, 10-11). The only thing that spared David from committing this deed was the gracious words of Abigail, Nabal's wife (vs. 23-35). There is, however, no indication that David's original intention was the will of God. More than likely, David's hand was sovereignly spared from carrying out such a foolish and unnecessary act (regardless of how discourteous Nabal may have been).

Another instance is the tragic account recorded in Judges 11:29-40. Jephthah made a tragic and inappropriate vow to the Lord. He sacrificed his only daughter in order to fulfill his vow to the Lord. What a terrible thing to do! We should not make rash, foolish or bad promises and if we do then we should not feel compelled to keep them. Just because something is recorded in Scripture does not mean it is approved by God.

Recorded or approved

In Acts 21:22-26 Paul took upon himself a vow. He shaved his head, purified himself according to Jewish custom and went into the temple, and even offered a sacrifice. He did this in order to demonstrate that he was not hostile to the Law or his Jewish heritage. This particular incident

---

[26] H. H. Rowley, cited in Bernard Ramm, *Protestant Biblical Interpretation: A Textbook of Hermeneutics*, (3rd edition, Grand Rapids, Mich.: Baker Book House, 1970), 154.

can hardly be normative for Christians today. In fact, there is no evidence that this was even considered normative for Jewish Christians living in the first century. It was only Paul and four other companions who undertook that vow.

What factors help us to discern whether an early apostolic church practice is normative for modern Christians?[27] How can we tell if something recorded in the New Testament is merely cultural or a distinctive apostolic practice which is normative for Christians of all ages? Admittedly, this is not always an easy question to answer. Christian theologians have not always found agreement. However, the following points may help the Bible student. We want to separate those early church practices, which were clearly cultural, and those, which are meant to be implemented by all believers of all eras. To begin with, we ought to separate things that were limited to the customs of the first-century era ~ such as wearing tunics, writing on parchments, etc.

There are distinctive practices and ministry patterns of the early church, which are normative. What is a distinctive, apostolic pattern and how can we tell what is distinctive and what is not? Briefly, a distinctive apostolic church pattern is a practice that often goes contrary to the culture of the day ~ for example, Jews and Gentiles meeting and eating together as one body. (Eph. 2:11-16) This was contrary to the religious custom of the day. Apostolic traditions countered both Jewish and pagan practices then prevalent in the Judeo and Greco-Roman worlds.[28] For example, the early Christians (in contrast to Judaism and the pagan mystery religions) had no need for temples or shrines. They did not have any need for special "holy men" or priests who would perform religious exercises on their behalf.[29]

Something that is intended to be normative is usually repeated within the New Testament. It is something that seems to have been the usual practice of the early Christian assemblies. There is a noticeable uniformity in basic church structure and practice, which appears to have been the mark of all apostolic churches. For example, the pattern of multiple participation may be found in Rom. 12:4-8; 1 Cor. 14:26; Eph. 4:11-16; 5:19; Col. 3:16; Heb. 10:24-25; 1 Pet.4:10-11. This indicates that there was a distinctive apostolic practice common to all the churches

---

[27] See the chapter in this book entitled "Finding the Normative in Acts for some principles and guidelines.

[28] It should, however, be noted that there are elements of continuity as well as discontinuity, in relation to Judaic practices, in early Christianity.

[29] This is not intended as a criticism of ordained ministers in the church today.

regardless of their geographical location.—1 Corinthians 4:16-17; 11:16; 14:33.

Rooted in Theology

Distinctive apostolic practices are rooted in theology. In other words, New Testament church forms were not meaningless or merely cultural, but instead, reflective of theological truth. They have a doctrinal basis. Thus using one cup and one bread in the Lord's Supper symbolizes unity in Christ. (1 Cor. 10:16-17) The important thing here is to observe the ordinance as commanded by the Lord ~ where, when and how are subordinate to *why* we do this. Allowing mutual participation in the assembly is the practical outworking of Paul's theology of the body. (1 Cor. 12:12-27; Eph. 4:16) But we must be careful not to sanctify *form*. It is *function* that is important ~ form is generally secondary.

A distinctive apostolic practice does not need to be explicitly commanded. Obviously, all the directives must be taken seriously. Things that are not explicitly commanded can still be authoritative for church practice. In fact, most church practices generally deemed necessary (to be faithful to apostolic teaching) are not commanded in the New Testament. For example, there is no direct command to gather weekly every Sunday. It is known that the early believers did regularly gather on the first day of the week (Sunday). However, there is no direct command to celebrate the Lord's Supper weekly. There is no direct command that every congregation has a plurality of elders and deacons. Yet these were clearly the distinctive apostolic patterns of the early church. Should they be practiced by churches today? There is no direct or explicit command that such patterns must be followed. Yet many churches would feel that they are less than faithful to the New Testament if they did not implement such ministry patterns.

The apostles did not need to preface all their words explicitly with direct commands. Most often the example or model which they set before us and encourage us to imitate is sufficient. (1 Cor. 4:16; 11:1-2, 16; 14:33; Phil. 3:17; 4:9; 1 Thess. 1:6-7; 2 Thess. 2:15) After all, Paul did explicitly say "Be imitators of me, as I am of Christ. Now I commend you because you remember me in everything and maintain the traditions even as I delivered them to you."—1 Corinthians 11:1-2.

It is important to be careful in exalting first-century Christianity as the ideal because not everything, which transpired, is *necessarily* the supreme example for churches today. While it is necessary to look for distinctive apostolic patterns, it must be borne in mind that no period of church history is infallible and to be emulated without question. In fact, we know that the early churches had many problems in belief and behavior.

In the Corinthian church, there was divisions and strife. Judaizers deceived the Galatian churches. Consider Christ's stern warnings to five of the seven churches of Asia Minor. (Rev. 2-3) While we must be faithful to apostolic ecclesiology, we should also be appreciative of those advances or contributions, which Christ has brought to his church through his servants in subsequent eras ~ such as Augustine, Luther, Calvin, Edwards, Carey and many others.

Do not Build a Doctrine on an Uncertain Textual Reading

We should not erect an entire teaching or system of theology upon a verse. Such an inverted pyramid is structurally unsafe. Christian theology should be built upon passages that exist in the original manuscripts. For instance, it would be wrong to defend the doctrine of the Trinity from the King James Version reading of 1 John 5:7 which says "For there are three that bear record in heaven, the Father, the Word, and the Holy Ghost: and these three are one." No known ancient manuscript can attest to this reading. Neither should we build a case for contemporary tongues and miraculous signs based upon Mark 16:15-18. Some of the earliest manuscripts do not include 16:9-20. Some Bible scholars do not believe that Mark wrote these verses, asserting they were added at a later date by some other author. The reason for this view is that the language used in these verses is different from the language used in the rest of the *Gospel of Mark*. The early church fathers mention this section being in *Mark* toward the end of the first century. Although Mark 16:9-20 is included in Bible publications it should be noted that it is an interpolation from a century after the author died and as such is not part of the original inspired canon of Scripture.[30]

---

[30] Christian Publishing House would suggest the following article: Was Mark 16:9-20 Written by Mark?

http://www.uasvbible.org/textual-mark-16-9-20

CHAPTER 5 Finding the Normative In Acts

Does the book of Acts simply record the history of the early church? Or does it also provide a blueprint for the church today? Do we read Acts as an interesting true story of how Christianity began, a story that gives us our roots and our identity or is it still normative for today? A passage or principle is normative if it can be regarded as applicable to us and required of us. This raises an important hermeneutical question ~ are we to read the book as though it were mainly prescriptive or purely descriptive? In other words, how relevant is Acts for the life of the twenty-first-century church?

The Problem

A quick guided tour of Acts will soon reveal what a huge question this is. The problem of normativeness stares the reader in the face on almost every page.

Chapter 1 shows the apostles are keen to fill the empty place left by Judas. Thus, the names of Joseph (called Barsabbas who was also called Justus) and Matthias are put forward. The choice is made by drawing lots (v. 26). Is that how we are to select church leaders today?

Chapter 2 opens in dramatic fashion. There was a sound like the blowing of a violent wind. Tongues of fire came to rest on all those who were present, and they began to speak in other tongues as the Spirit enabled them. Can these phenomena be expected wherever the gospel breaks new ground as it does in chapters 8, 10 and 19? Can they still be expected to happen whenever revival takes place?[31]

Later in the same chapter, Peter preaches a very effective sermon ~ that is his sermon on the day of Pentecost. Does this sermon establish the groundwork for apostolic preaching? Is it the paradigm for all future preaching or was Peter addressing a unique situation?

Further on in Acts 2, we are told something about the three thousand who were converted by Peter's sermon, "And they devoted

---

[31] I do not intend to deal with cessationist or continuationist positions in relation to the "controversial" gifts. Cessationists argue that the gifts of prophecy, speaking in tongues and miraculous (dramatic and instantaneous healings, including raising people from the dead) ceased in the first century. They contend that they were a special dispensation for that time in order to demonstrate the power of God in the formative years of the church's history, thus allowing the church to become established. Continuationists, such as Pentecostals and Charismatic believers assert that these gifts are still operative in the church today.

themselves to the apostles' teaching and to the fellowship, to the breaking of bread and to prayer." (v. 42) Are these intended to be the basics of Christian worship? Are they valid for all time? These believers also had everything in common. They sold their possessions and goods to give to anyone in need. (vs. 44-45) Does that mean that the sharing of property is mandatory for believers today? We are also told that the original church at Jerusalem met both "in the temple courts" and "from house to house." (v. 46) Does that mean that the church today should have both larger worship services and home groups? Is that the biblical pattern?

In chapter 3, Peter and John heal a cripple sitting outside the temple. Throughout Acts, there are many such healings and miracles. Should we still expect the same kind of dramatic healings today?

In chapter 4, the Sanhedrin threatens the apostles Peter and John, and so the church calls for a time of prayer. Is calling a prayer meeting at a time of need normative? At the end of chapter 4, the believers are again selling property and sharing goods. (as they did in Acts 2) Is a pattern developing here?

In chapter five, in the deaths of Ananias and Sapphira, we have an instance of church discipline of the most drastic kind. Does the Holy Spirit still take such a dim view of lying to a church leader and might God still act in the same way? Later in chapter 5, the apostles are arrested and put in the public jail. However, during the night, an angel of the Lord opens the doors of the jail and brings them out (vs. 18-19). Could God still give gospel-preachers miraculous jail breaks in our own time?[32]

In chapter 6, the apostles vow to devote themselves to prayer and the ministry of the word. (v. 4) Should the same priority apply to ministers and elders today? At the same time, the apostles also told the church to choose seven men who were known to be full of the Spirit and wisdom to take care of the daily distribution of food. When these men had been chosen, the apostles prayed and laid their hands on them. Is this a good way to appoint deacons and other church leaders? Should deacons be men (not women) and should the number always be seven?

In chapter 8, the Samaritans received the Holy Spirit after they believed and were baptized. Could this also happen today? In v. 29 of this chapter the Spirit said to Philip, "Go to that chariot and stay near it." Can we still expect such direct communication? The Ethiopian eunuch was baptized immediately after Jesus was preached to him. Should we follow this example and baptize people as soon as they respond to the gospel?

---

[32] Perhaps the question *could* God do it is not the right way to phrase it, the real question might be *does* God do it?

Chapter 9 starts with the conversion of the apostle Paul. Should we still expect "Damascus Road" conversions today? Or should we look for factors here that are essential to every conversion?

The way that Peter came to preach at the house of Cornelius was a masterpiece of divine choreography. Does God still make special arrangements like this for the sake of the propagation of the gospel?

At the end of chapter 11 the disciples at Antioch provided help for their brothers in Judea during a time of famine, and they sent their gift to the elders by Barnabas and Saul. Is this a good precedent to follow?

Does God still deal with rulers as he did with Herod Agrippa I who did not give praise to God and was eaten by worms and died? (Acts 12:23) For Paul's first missionary journey Antioch served as the sending church. Is this just a good practice or should it be policy ~ i.e. normative?

Do miracles of judgment, like the blinding of Elymas the magician in Acts 13, still occur today?

Paul's first recorded sermon was preached in the synagogue at Pisidian Antioch. It is studded with Old Testament quotations and works its way through the redemptive history of Israel. Could this be a model for today's preachers? In his missionary work, Paul made the synagogue his first port of call in every town that had one. Would this be a helpful strategy for mission agencies to follow?

Towards the end of the first missionary journey, Paul and Barnabas appointed elders in every church with prayer and fasting. Should that also be the pattern for us?

Does the Jerusalem Council of Acts 15 provide a biblical rationale for synods, general assemblies, and other church councils? The decision of the council is stated thus ~ "You are to abstain from food sacrificed to idols, from blood, from the meat of strangled animals and from sexual immorality" (Acts 15:29) ~ does this still apply to Gentile believers today? Should Christians today avoid all of these things, all of the time? Should Christians today avoid some of these things, all of the time? Should Christians today avoid some of these things, some of the time? The Jerusalem Council conveyed its decision to the Gentile believers by way of a letter. Is that still the best way to convey the decisions of governing bodies?

Does God always overrule disputes between Christian leaders so that the church benefits as much as it did in the case of Barnabas and Paul (Acts 15:36-41)?

The contrast between Lydia's conversion (Acts 16:14) and the Philippian jailer's (Acts 16:27-34) is quite marked. Is this a tacit warning against stereotyping conversion experiences?

In Ephesus, Paul placed his hands on twelve former disciples of John the Baptist. The Holy Spirit came upon them, and they spoke in tongues and prophesied (Acts 19:6). Does this mean that tongues and prophecy are a "second blessing" experience after conversion? At Troas, the church came together on the first day of the week (Acts 20:7). Does this mean that public worship should always be on the first day of the week? In Muslim countries, believers often meet on Friday.

Paul's address to the Ephesian elders is perhaps the closest that Acts comes to recording a sermon addressed specifically to believers, as we do in our worship services. To what extent should this be a pattern for our own preaching? Alternatively, does the point lie elsewhere, e.g. in the way a pastor is to care for his flock?

In Acts 25, Paul appealed to Caesar (vs. 10-12, 25). Nowadays should Christians appeal to a higher court if they cannot get justice or satisfaction from a lower court?

At the height of the storm at sea in Acts 27, Paul gets a message from an angel to the effect that all the passengers and crew will be saved, but that the ship and its cargo will be lost (vs. 22-26). Can we still expect to receive such accurate angelic messages?

In the last chapter of Acts, on the island of Malta, a snake fastened itself on Paul's hand, but he shook the snake off into the fire and suffered no ill effects. (Acts 28:3-5) So should Christians today be expected to deal with serpents in the same way?

We cannot answer all these questions. It is beyond our scope to give exhaustive solutions to the problems raised. However, let me try to provide principles that can be used to help us answer these questions. We want to try to get a handle on the issue of what is normative in Acts. We can use three principles that will be helpful in specific cases.

The Principle of Non-Contradiction

First, is the principle of non-contradiction. We cannot claim to have discovered an absolute in Acts if it leads to a contradiction in either doctrine or practice. For example, how does the church select its leaders? To replace Judas the apostles cast lots. (Acts 1:26) To discover the seven who should wait at tables they handed the matter over to the church. They let the church make the decision, which they then ratified. (Acts 6:1-6) Towards the end of the first missionary journey, Paul and Barnabas appointed elders after prayer and fasting. (Acts 14:23) These are all very different approaches, and they are also mutually exclusive. We cannot cast lots, delegate and appoint all at the same time! Therefore, none of these should be elevated to an absolute.

This principle of non-contradiction applies not only to practice but to doctrine as well. When Peter had finished preaching his Pentecost sermon, the crowd responded in a way that would be the envy of every preacher. They said, "What shall we do?" Peter answered, "Repent and be baptized...and you will receive the gift of the Holy Spirit" (Acts 2:38). It sounds very straightforward. First, you repent and are baptized, and then you receive the Holy Spirit. In other words, repentance and baptism come before the receiving of the Holy Spirit. However, before this is elevated into a doctrine, it would be wise to check it out in the light of the unfolding story of Acts.

In chapter 8, we read about the conversion of the Samaritans, and sure enough, the hypothesis holds. At the preaching of Philip they believe and are baptized. (Acts 8:12) Only after the apostles Peter and John arrive do they receive the Holy Spirit. (Acts 8:17) Before we think we have proved our point, however, we need to keep reading. In Acts 10, in the case of Cornelius and his household, the Holy Spirit came on all of them while Peter was still preaching. (Acts 10:44) As a result, they broke out in tongues and started praising God. Only then did Peter order them to be baptized. (Acts 10:48) In Acts 19, we meet a dozen or so disciples of John the Baptist in Ephesus. They too were baptized and received the Holy Spirit. In addition, it seems that in this case the two events were almost simultaneous. (vs. 5-6) At least there does not seem to have been an interval between their water baptism and the giving of the Holy Spirit.

All four instances are therefore different enough that we need to be cautious. We cannot take Peter's words - "Repent and be baptized...and you will receive the gift of the Holy Spirit" as the basis of an order of salvation experience that is relevant to every believer. It is always dangerous to base a doctrine on isolated texts from Acts. Fee and Stuart comment on this:

> Luke's interest does not seem to be on standardizing things, bringing everything into uniformity. When he records individual conversions there are usually two elements included: water baptism and the gift of the Spirit. But these can be in reverse order, with or without the laying on of hands, with or without the mention of tongues, and scarcely ever with a specific mention of repentance, even after what Peter says in 2:38-

39...Such diversity probably means that no specific example is being set forth as the model Christian experience.[33]

Prescriptive or Descriptive?

The second principle, which helps find the normative in Acts is to differentiate between what is *prescriptive* and what is *descriptive*. When an action is commanded, it is far more likely to be normative than when it is merely described. Fee and Stuart state the matter even more strongly ~ perhaps too strongly. They operate on the assumption that, "...unless Scripture explicitly tells us we must do something, what is merely narrated or described can never function in a normative way."[34] For example, it is simply there for the record that Paul made the synagogue his first stop in every town that had one. Nowhere does he command others to do so. In a similar vein, we are told that at Pentecost believers sold their possessions and goods so that they could alleviate the needs of others. Nowhere are they told to do so.

Repentance and Baptism

Compare these examples to Peter's call to the Jerusalem crowd to repent. (Acts 2:38) This command occurs again and again in Acts. He issues the same command in his sermon in chapter 3, "Repent, then, and turn to God, so that your sins may be wiped out and that times of refreshing may come from the Lord." (v.19) In Samaria, he challenges Simon Magus, "Repent of this wickedness and pray to the Lord. Perhaps he will forgive you for having such a thought in your heart." (Acts 8:22) At Athens, Paul declared, "God now commands all men everywhere to repent." (Acts 17:30) In his defense before King Agrippa Paul gave a summary of his ministry to both Jews and Gentiles, "I preached that they should repent and turn to God and prove their repentance by their deeds." (Acts 26:20) Therefore, when Peter tells the crowd at Pentecost to repent this is a universal command. He is not just telling Jews in Jerusalem to repent of their involvement in the death of Jesus. This is a command to all people everywhere. It is normative. The same goes for the command to be baptized which he issues in the same breath. Throughout Acts, people are baptized, Jews and Gentiles alike. "Repent

---

[33] Gordon D. Fee and Douglas Stuart, *How to Read the Bible for All It's Worth: A Guide to Understanding the Bible*, (Grand Rapids: Zondervan, 1982), 92.

[34] Gordon D. Fee and Douglas Stuart, *How to Read the Bible for All It's Worth*, 97.

and be baptized" is, therefore, a universal command that should be proclaimed as much by us as it was by Peter at Pentecost.

Dietary Issues and Sexual Morality

What about the verse, "You are to abstain from food sacrificed to idols, from blood, from the meat of strangled animals and from sexual immorality." (Acts 15:29) This command occurs more than once. It is addressed specifically to Gentile believers. But does this still apply to Gentile believers today? This was a decision made by the Jerusalem Council in Acts 15 and was addressed specifically to Gentile Christians. For good measure, this prohibition is stated on three separate occasions. (cf. Acts 15:20; 21:25) So it must be very important, but is it normative in the same way as Peter's command to repent and be baptized? Should pastors and preachers tell their congregations to abstain from the same things as those Gentile believers in Acts 15? Are there really certain meats which Christians shouldn't eat today? We can keep on reading in Acts, but that will not answer our question. We need to cast our eyes further afield, and that will also bring us to our next principle.

Reinforcement in Other Parts of the New Testament

The third principle that helps us find the normative in Acts is that of reinforcement in other parts of the New Testament. In other words, a command (or even a practice) in Acts carries more weight if it is repeated elsewhere in the New Testament. Here we need to think particularly of the teaching of Jesus and the Epistles. This is where we are more likely to come across timeless truths and normative commands. So let us put the Jerusalem decree through this grid and see what the outcome might be. John Stott says:

> The purpose of God in Scripture should be sought primarily in its didactic rather than its descriptive parts. More precisely, we should look for it in the teaching of Jesus, and in the sermons and writings of the apostles, rather than in the purely narrative portions of the Acts. What is described in Scripture as having happened to others is not necessarily intended for us...What is descriptive is valuable only in so far as it is interpreted by what is didactic.[35]

---

[35] John R. W. Stott, *Baptism and Fullness: The Work of the Holy Spirit Today* (2nd ed.; Leicester: Inter-Varsity Press, 1975), 15.

We begin with the simplest example ~ the warning to abstain from sexual immorality. The word πορνεία (*porneia*) which refers to sexual immorality could be used in a more restricted sense. F. F. Bruce says:

> The most elementary teaching given to converts from paganism almost certainly made it clear that fornication and similar practices were incompatible with the Christian way. Even so, the Jerusalem leaders may have felt that no harm would be done by underlining this in the decree. But fornication could bear a more technical sense of marital union within the prohibited degrees of consanguinity or affinity laid down in the Hebrew "law of holiness" (Leviticus 18:6-18).[36]

Consanguinity refers to determining whether a couple can marry. Some United States jurisdictions forbid first cousins to marry, while others limit the prohibition to brothers, sisters, mothers, fathers, aunts and uncles.

Outside of the Jerusalem decree, Acts never again refers to immorality. But this warning is repeated time and again in the New Testament ~ in the teaching of Jesus (Mt. 5:32; 15:19; 19:9), in the Epistles (Rom. 1:29; 1 Cor. 6:13, 18; 7:2; Gal. 5:19; Eph. 5:3; Col. 3:3; 1 Thess. 4:3) and in the book of Revelation. (2: 21; 9: 21) Throughout the New Testament both Jesus and the apostles take a dim view of immorality and speak against it repeatedly and consistently. So it may be said with certainty this part of the Jerusalem decree was intended to apply to all believers at all times and in all places. As such it applies to us, and it is required of us. In other words, it is normative.

After this, it begins to get more difficult. There are no more references to abstaining from blood and the meat of strangled animals either in Acts or anywhere else in the New Testament. This instruction concerning abstention is confined entirely to the Jerusalem decree. So what do we do with it? Can we eat any meats or do we have to be selective? Should we ask the butcher (or the supermarket manager/purchasing officer) if the meat we are buying is from a strangled animal?

Should we eat only kosher foods that conform to the regulations of כַּשְׁרוּת (*kashrut*) Jewish dietary law? In the early church context the eating of such foods would be particularly offensive to Jews. F. F. Bruce says:

> Eating with blood was absolutely taboo for Jews: it is expressly forbidden in Leviticus 17:10-14 and even earlier, in the

---

[36] F. F. Bruce, *Paul: Apostle of the Free Spirit* (rev. ed.; Carlisle: Paternoster, 1992), 185.

commandments enjoined on Noah and his family (Genesis 9:4). People who had been brought up in the Jewish way of life could not be expected to accept such food at Gentile tables.[37]

That brings us to the last requirement of the Jerusalem Council. The Gentile believers were also to abstain from food sacrificed to idols. This is an issue that comes up again in the New Testament. Paul has an extensive discussion on it in 1 Corinthians 8-10. It is a question that the Corinthians have raised in a letter to Paul. The significant point here is that they raised this with him long after the decision that was reached by the Jerusalem Council. Probably from six to eight years later ~ yet Paul does not quote the Jerusalem decree to the church at Corinth. Even though he was present when the decision was taken and he was one of those who conveyed it to the church at Antioch.

What Paul does is very enlightening. He does not appeal to the decision made at Jerusalem. Rather he takes a very pastoral approach. He asks the Corinthians to remember those with weaker consciences. Then there follows a nuanced discussion and in this discussion he shows how they are to take account of their weaker brothers. Essentially, he makes three points. First, never eat in an idol temple ~ that could be spiritually damaging for your weaker brother. Second, if you buy meat at the meat market don't ask any questions ~ what you don't know won't hurt you, and it won't hurt anyone else either. Third, if an unbeliever invites you to dinner don't ask any questions. But if he tells you that this is meat that has been sacrificed to an idol, don't eat it. Paul's directions have therefore clearly gone beyond the Jerusalem decree.

Why does he feel free to ignore or at least modify what the council agreed? Does he take matters into his own hands? Not really. The Jerusalem decree was not intended to be forever binding. It was a temporary measure designed to appease the Jewish believers who had lost the debate over Gentile circumcision. The letter that contained the decree was addressed to "the Gentile believers in Antioch, Syria and Cilicia." (Acts 21:23) It had only limited application and was designed to be temporary. The gospel had now moved on (or rather people's understanding of the gospel had progressed). The Jerusalem decree did not apply in the same way to the Corinthians as it had to the Gentile believers in Antioch, Syria and Cilicia. It had permanent aspects like the warning against sexual immorality, but it was not intended to be permanent or binding in all its proscriptions.

---

[37] F. F. Bruce, *Paul: Apostle of the Free Spirit*, 185-86.

An Important Principle

So we can eat anything from the butchers. But we might need to be sensitive if we are having a meal with a young Jewish believer or, indeed a Muslim. In the example of the Jerusalem decree, we have identified a very important principle. A command or a practice in Acts can only be considered normative if reinforced elsewhere in the New Testament. The command to abstain from sexual immorality is permanently valid as it is repeated again and again. The command to abstain from meat offered to idols is modified in the light of the different situation in Corinth. The commands to abstain from blood and the meat of strangled animals are never mentioned again. These will only be relevant in situations that are very similar to the situation in Acts 15. For example, if you are working among Jewish people who eat only kosher foods.

The command, "you must not eat meat that has its lifeblood still in it" (Gen. 9:4) was given to Noah, and it predates the laws of Moses. It cannot be argued that it has universal validity. It is another dietary law that is no longer binding because of the completed work of Christ, which abolished the ritual law.

In his own ministry, Jesus declared all foods clean. (Mk. 7:19) For this reason, Peter could be told to "kill and eat" (Acts 10:13) and not to "call anything impure that God has made clean." (Acts 10:15) For the same reason, Paul could say, "I am fully convinced that no food is unclean of itself."—Romans 14:14.

The death of Jesus radically altered all the Old Testament food laws. Although concessions still needed to be made to those who had tender consciences on the issue. (Rom. 14:1-8) None of the dietary laws remain absolutely binding on Christians today.

Norm or Normative?

The Bible contains teachings and mandates that apply to all cultural situations, but it also contains teachings and mandates that apply only to particular situations. It is not always easy to determine which is which, and hence there is not always consensus among Christian communities about what is universal and what is particular. What is merely cultural for then and there? What is universal and applicable to all cultures and times, including here and now? What is the norm and what is normative? The norm refers to something that was normal then and there but is not necessarily expected to apply in the here and now. Normative refers not only to the normal practice then and there but also to principles that apply to the here and now. Some biblical commands are directed to

49

specific situations but may also be be normative. Consider the following passage from the book of Acts:

> And they devoted themselves to the apostles' teaching and the fellowship, to the breaking of bread and the prayers. And awe came upon every soul, and many wonders and signs were being done through the apostles. And all who believed were together and had all things in common. And they were selling their possessions and belongings and distributing the proceeds to all, as any had need. And day by day, attending the temple together and breaking bread in their homes, they received their food with glad and generous hearts, praising God and having favor with all the people. And the Lord added to their number day by day those who were being saved.—Acts 2:42-47.

Why is v.42 considered to be normative and vs.44-46 considered to be the norm for then but not normative for now? Why do we preach the importance of being devoted to apostolic teaching, fellowship, breaking of bread and prayer, while neglecting to emphasize selling our possessions and distributing the proceeds to the needy? The reason is connected to the eschatological hope of first-century believers that the second coming of Christ was imminent. They lived in the light of that understanding. Two millennia later believers accept the truth of Christ's return as something that is taught in Scripture but is not, rightly or wrongly, so obsessed or confident that it is something about to happen at any moment.

Although it is important to be devoted to apostolic teaching, fellowship, breaking of bread and prayer it must be said that this passage from Acts is not a proof text for such attitudes and actions in the church. In other words, it does not directly teach that these things must be observed. It is descriptive rather than prescriptive. Obviously, this hermeneutical understanding of the text will have implications for homiletics (preaching). In preaching the importance of being devoted to apostolic teaching, fellowship, breaking of bread and prayer then it becomes important to use texts that clearly direct believers to do so. It is still very useful to use the Acts passage as an example of a thriving, vibrant church. But bear in mind that to do so while separating the first part of the passage from the latter part needs some careful thought and explanation. One can abuse a text by using it to teach something wrong (i.e. not the intended meaning) but one can also abuse a text by using it to teach something right ~ i.e. not the intended meaning in the text, though such a meaning may be taught elsewhere in Scripture.

A Purely Descriptive Statement

This is a purely descriptive statement. There is nothing prescriptive about it. There is no imperative, no warning and no prohibition. It is just a description pure and simple. It is an observation made by Luke the historian. It is part of his narrative. Here you have the essential elements of a worship service ~ teaching, fellowship, the Lord's Supper, and prayer. But the foundation for such activity is not taken *just* from this one verse of narrative. All of these elements can be found again in the Epistles. Here we have in seed form what comes to full flower elsewhere in the New Testament, especially in 1 Corinthians.

When it comes to possessions what happens when we read the rest of Acts and the rest of the New Testament? This idyllic situation that we have in Jerusalem is never repeated in Acts or anywhere else. Some have suggested that it was an experiment gone wrong. That later the church in Jerusalem had to be bailed out, first by the church at Antioch and later by the churches that Paul established in Greece and Asia Minor. E. M. Blaiklock says, "...the poverty of the Jerusalem church, which later called for worldwide charity, may have been occasioned by this over-hasty dissipation of capital."[38] But that view is not only uncharitable; it also misses the point. In later years the church in Jerusalem was poor. But it was not because of financial mismanagement but because of famine and persecution. Paul writes very eloquently about this to the Corinthians. The classic chapters on this are 2 Corinthians 8 and 9. There he tells the Christians at Corinth to give systematically, generously and cheerfully. He does not tell them to sell private property. Perhaps some of them did so, but we are never told. To the Ephesians, Paul gives this command, "He who has been stealing must steal no longer, but must work, doing something useful with his own hands, that he may have something to share with those in need." (Eph. 4:28) In 1 Timothy, he has some direct challenges to the rich:

> Command those who are rich in this present world not to be arrogant nor to put their hope in wealth, which is so uncertain, but to put their hope in God, who richly provides us with everything for our enjoyment. Command them to do good, to be rich in good deeds, and to be generous and willing to share.—1 Timothy 6:17-18.

Notice that here too there is nothing about selling property. He is not saying, "Let's go back to the paradigm of the early Jerusalem church."

---

[38] E. M. Blaiklock *The Acts of the Apostles: An Historical Commentary*, (London: Tyndale, 1959), 69.

But he is telling them to be generous and to be willing to share. That is what is normative for Christians today. That is what is applicable to us and required from us. In the affluent church of the West, we are to be generous and willing to share. If that means selling property, so be it. But that is not part of the command. The basic principle is generosity and willingness to share. John Stott says:

> Certainly the generosity and mutual care of those early Christians are to be followed, for the New Testament commands us many times to love and serve one another, and to be generous (even sacrificial) in our giving. But to argue from the practice of the early Jerusalem church that all private ownership is abolished among Christians not only cannot be maintained from Scripture but is plainly contradicted by the apostle Peter in the same context (Acts 5:4) and by the apostle Paul elsewhere. (e.g. I Tim. 6:17)[39]

Now let us come back for a moment to what Luke said about worship in the Jerusalem church after Pentecost. Not only does he report that, "...they devoted themselves to the apostles' teaching and to the fellowship, to the breaking of bread and to prayer" (Acts 2:42) he also adds later that they met together in the temple courts and in their homes (Acts 2:46). Is this also to be a model for us? Like those early believers, should we meet in larger gatherings at church on Sundays and in smaller groups in people's homes during the week? In the early church in Jerusalem, they met together in the temple courts and broke bread in their homes. However, it does not seem to be a pattern that is repeated anywhere else. For a start, only Jerusalem had the temple. And in many situations, the only place where the church could meet was in people's homes.

Handle with Care

Preachers need to be careful in the way they handle Acts. We must not see directives where none are given. Proper hermeneutics is required before we proclaim some command or practice to be normative. So let us first apply these three hermeneutical principles that we have discovered so far. First, we need to consider the principle of non-contradiction. Does the practice or doctrine we think we have discovered contradict another teaching or practice in Acts? Second, we need to ask whether we are dealing with a command or a description. Third, is the command or practice reinforced in other parts of the New Testament? This is the most

---

[39] John R. W Stott, *Baptism and Fullness: The Work of the Holy Spirit Today*, (2nd ed.; Leicester: Inter-Varsity Press, 1975), 16.

important principle because it is not the nature of narrative to be normative. Acts is essentially a narrative. A story may have a moral but not every detail implies a command to obey or an example to follow.

CHAPTER 6 Keys to Understanding

Recognize the Christocentric focus of the Bible

The New Testament writers primarily viewed the Old Testament as Christological documents. They understood the Hebrew Scriptures as ultimately pointing to the person of Christ and the redemptive-historical fulfillment that he would bring:

- And He took the twelve aside and said to them, "Behold, we are going up to Jerusalem, and all things which are written through the prophets about the Son of Man will be accomplished." (Lk. 18:31)

- And beginning with Moses and with all the prophets, He explained to them the things concerning Himself in all the Scriptures. (Lk. 24:27)

- Philip found Nathanael and said to him, "We have found Him of whom Moses in the Law and also the Prophets wrote, Jesus of Nazareth, the son of Joseph." (Jn. 1:45)

- See Jn. 5:46; Acts 2:30-31; 3:18; 10:43; 17:2-3; 1 Cor. 10:4; 15:3-4; 1 Pet. 1:10-11.

This does not mean that every text of Scripture in the Old Testament speaks directly or explicitly of Christ. But every text of Old Testament Scripture is part of the one story which has its ultimate focus in Jesus. As the late New Testament scholar F. F. Bruce, has written:

> In Jesus the promise is confirmed, the covenant is renewed, the prophecies are fulfilled, the law is vindicated, salvation is brought near, sacred history has reached its climax, the perfect sacrifice has been offered and accepted, the great High Priest over the household of God has taken His seat at God's right hand, the Prophet like Moses has been raised up, the Son of David reigns, the kingdom of God has been inaugurated, the Son of Man has received dominion from the Ancient of Days, the Servant of the Lord, having been smitten to death for His people's transgression and borne the sin of many, has accomplished the divine purpose, has seen light after the travail

of His soul and is now exalted and extolled and made very high.[40]

The *Sensus Plenior*

The term *Sensus Plenior* (fuller sense) helps the Bible student understand that Old Testament history has a deeper and more far-reaching meaning. It adds additional insight to historical-grammatical exegesis. *Sensus Plenior*, by definition, means God's intended meaning in Scripture. This may or may not have been discerned by the human author. But it is made clear by the subsequent revelation of the Holy Spirit in the New Testament. As William LaSor points out, "...the author does not intentionally convey the *Sensus Plenior* to his hearers. But at a later date, in the light of further revelation, the fuller meaning becomes clear to readers under the influence of the Spirit, who inspired the original author."[41]

This should not be seen as a denial of the validity of the historical-grammatical method. Neither is it an endorsement of allegorical or mystical exegesis. When guided by proper controls, the principle of *Sensus Plenior* helps us to see the divine intention. It helps us see the deeper theological purpose behind certain events and persons of biblical history. These are not arbitrary meanings discovered by a creative interpreter. They are not just chosen or determined at random. They are not based solely on personal wishes, feelings, or perceptions. After all, we want objective facts, reasons, and principles to guide us. But the *Sensus Plenior* offers us insights of New Testament writers who were uniquely granted such insight by the Holy Spirit. As the theologian, Louis Berkhof, has stated:

> The real meaning of Scripture does not always lie on the surface. There is no truth in the assertion that the intent of the secondary authors (God being the primary author), determined by the grammatical-historical method, always exhausts the sense of Scripture, and represents in all its fullness the meaning of the Holy Spirit.[42]

---

[40] F. F. Bruce, *New Testament Development of Old Testament Themes*, (Wipf & Stock, 2004), 21.

[41] William LaSor, "Interpretation of Prophecy," *Hermeneutics*, Bernard Ramm, (Baker, 1971), 108.

[42] Louis Berkhof, *Principles of Biblical Interpretation* (Grand Rapids, Michigan: Baker Book House, 1950), 59-60.

For example, King David's shocking betrayal by a close friend, as recorded in Psalm 41:9 was not a literal prediction or direct messianic prophecy. Nevertheless, Jesus applied this historic experience and lamentation to himself. (Jn. 13:18) Thus, Jesus elevated David's unfortunate betrayal to a type, which was fulfilled in the betrayal of Christ by Judas. Just as David was betrayed by a close friend, so also the greater David, the true King of Israel, is likewise betrayed. So Jesus unfolded Psalm 41:9 in a deeper, Christological sense.

Hosea 11:1 says "Out of Egypt I called My Son," which is understood as a reference to the future Messiah. The prophet was not looking forward to the distant future. Rather he was looking to the past when God brought the nation of Israel out of their Egyptian bondage. Yet Matthew 2:15, understands Hosea 11:1 as having its ultimate reference and fulfillment in Jesus. Thus, Matthew, under the guidance of the Holy Spirit, sees the deeper significance and Christological sense of Hosea 11:1. He tries to teach us that the meaning of Israel's history is fully revealed in the life and mission of Jesus Christ.

Take, as another example, the words of Jeremiah, "A voice is heard in Ramah, lamentation, and bitter weeping. Rachel is weeping for her children; she refuses to be comforted for her children because they are no more." (Jer. 31:15). In its historical context, this refers to the deportation of the Jews to Babylon where, symbolically, Rachel, as the mother of Israel, is pictured weeping. However, Matthew sees this weeping as "fulfilled" in the wailing of those mothers whose children were slaughtered in Bethlehem by Herod (Mt. 2:17-18). Thus, Matthew understands the words of Jeremiah 31:15 as having ultimate and fuller meaning in the events of Jesus' early life. According to Hans K. La Rondelle:

> Matthew interprets many crucial events in Israel's history as a foreshadowing of Messianic fulfillments. In the life of Christ, the fuller meaning of Israel's sacred history is brought to light. In this way, Matthew tries to confirm the Christian faith that Jesus is the Messiah of Israel and that God has achieved His goal in His salvation-history with Israel...In summary, the New Testament reveals a multiplex, Christ-centered approach to the Old Testament, which is theologically richer and more comprehensive than the hermeneutic of literalism.[43]

It should be noted that not all scholars accept the notion of *Sensus Plenior* as valid. Some see such New Testament uses of the Old Testament

---

[43] Hans K. La Rondelle, *The Israel of God in Prophecy: Principles of Prophetic Interpretation* (Andrews University Press, 1983), 74, 77.

as merely analogies and parallels. They would argue that the gospel writers were not attempting to draw the fuller meaning from the verses they cited and applied to Jesus. Instead, they were merely showing analogies or similarities between Old and New Testament events. They say that this was a practice which would have been appreciated by Matthew's Jewish readers. But the New Testament writers brought forth the fuller meaning of certain verses which were divinely intended to have a broader range of meaning.

For instance, the promise spoken to Abraham, "...in your offspring shall all the nations of the earth be blessed." (Gen. 22:18) This had a much broader significance than at first appears. Later revelation would eventually discover this broader significance, "Now the promises were made to Abraham and to his offspring. It does not say, 'And to offsprings,' referring to many, but referring to one, 'And to your offspring,' who is Christ.'"—Galatians 3:16.

In a passage, concerning the plot to kill Jesus the apostle John records the words of the High Priest Caiaphas:

Many of the Jews, therefore, who had come with Mary and had seen what he did, believed in him, but some of them went to the Pharisees and told them what Jesus had done. So the chief priests and the Pharisees gathered the Council and said, "What are we to do? For this man performs many signs. If we let him go on like this, everyone will believe in him, and the Romans will come and take away both our place and our nation." But one of them, Caiaphas, who was high priest that year, said to them, "You know nothing at all. Nor do you understand that it is better for you that one man should die for the people, not that the whole nation should perish." He did not say this of his own accord, but being high priest that year he prophesied that Jesus would die for the nation, and not for the nation only, but also to gather into one the children of God who are scattered abroad. So from that day on they made plans to put him to death. Jesus therefore no longer walked openly among the Jews, but went from there to the region near the wilderness, to a town called Ephraim, and there he stayed with the disciples. Now the Passover of the Jews was at hand, and many went up from the country to Jerusalem before the Passover to purify themselves. They were looking for Jesus and saying to one another as they stood in the temple, "What do you think? That he will not come to the feast at all?" Now the chief priests and the Pharisees had given orders that if anyone knew where he was, he should let them know, so that they might arrest him.

Here Caiaphas explains the messianic meaning of prophecy concerning Christ. John's comments concerning the words of Caiaphas should be noted here. According to the apostle, the words of Caiaphas also had a much deeper meaning and significance than at first appeared. Under the inspiration of the Holy Spirit, he was able to see the divine intention in Caiaphas' proposed solution to deal with Jesus.

It is not the modern exegete who employs the *Sensus Plenior* of Scripture. It is solely the New Testament authors who were divinely guided to see the Holy Spirit's meaning in specific Old Testament passages. As Robertson McQuilkin states:

> Whatever position a person takes on the question of a hidden, secondary meaning in prophetic utterances or a fuller meaning intended from the beginning, Jesus Christ or the inspired writers are the only ones who can designate that secondary or fuller meaning. When Christ spoke, He had every right to interpret the author. The same may be said of those apostles He authorized to reveal God's will through the New Testament.[44]

Poetic Parallelism

The biblical writers were not dispassionate authors who merely transcribed information. Their world was one in which people expressed their thoughts in vivid language. Their emotions were engaged. One of the more common forms of aesthetic expression in Scripture is poetic parallelism. There are different types of poetic parallelism ~ synonymous, antithetical, synthetic, climactic and chiasmic. Poetic parallelism is usually observed in a passage where the second line repeats or contrasts the thoughts of the first line. The purpose of parallelism is to give intensity and force to the subject under discussion. This repetition or contrast makes the reader more aware of the author's argument or flow of thought, which creates a deeper impression.

Poetry appears in the Psalms, the prophets, and is the form of Proverbs. It should be noted that there can be prophetic elements in the psalms (e.g. Ps. 22 a cameo of the crucifixion and psalm 41:9, cited by Jesus concerning Judas). Poetic parallelism repeats and develops ideas.

---

[44] Robertson McQuilkin, *Understanding and Applying the Bible* (Chicago: Moody Press, Rev. edition 1992), 46.

Poetry reaches the mind through the emotions. Within the structure of parallelism, often, the second line will relate to the first line in some way. The second line may contrast, reinforce, or develop the first line. Very often the King James Version of the Bible better represents poetic parallelism in its style of presentation. For this reason, the quotations used to illustrate poetic parallelism (below) are from the King James Version. Some basic examples are given below.

Synonymous Parallelism

Synonymous means the same, or almost the same, as another word in the same language.

Proverbs 1:24-28

24 Because I have called and you refused to listen,
  have stretched out my hand and no one has heeded,
25 because you have ignored all my counsel
  and would have none of my reproof,
26 I also will laugh at your calamity;
  I will mock when terror strikes you,
27 when terror strikes you like a storm
  and your calamity comes like a whirlwind,
  when distress and anguish come upon you.
28 Then they will call upon me, but I will not answer;
  they will seek me diligently but will not find me.

Proverbs 6:2

2 if you are snared in the words of your mouth,
caught in the words of your mouth,

Matthew 7:7-8

7 "Ask, and it will be given to you; seek, and you will find; knock, and it will be opened to you. 8 For everyone who asks receives, and the one who seeks finds, and to the one who knocks it will be opened.

Antithetical Parallelism

This form of parallelism expresses the complete opposite by contrasting.

Proverbs 10:7-11

7 The memory of the righteous is a blessing,
  but the name of the wicked will rot.
8 The wise of heart will receive commandments,

but a babbling fool will come to ruin.
⁹ Whoever walks in integrity walks securely,
   but he who makes his ways crooked will be found out.
¹⁰ Whoever winks the eye causes trouble,
   and a babbling fool will come to ruin.
¹¹ The mouth of the righteous is a fountain of life,
   but the mouth of the wicked conceals violence.

Proverbs 15:17

¹⁷ Better is a dinner of herbs where love is
than a fattened ox and hatred with it.

Matthew 10:32-33

³² So everyone who acknowledges me before men, I also will acknowledge before my Father who is in heaven, ³³ but whoever denies me before men, I also will deny before my Father who is in heaven.

Synthetic Parallelism

In synthetic parallelism, the second or third lines of the unit are not synonymous or antithetical to the first line but advance the thought in a variety of other ways. For example, one of the lines may give a comparison to illuminate the other:

Psalm 103:13

¹³ As a father shows compassion to his children,
so the Lord shows compassion to those who fear him.

Other lines of synthetic parallelism relate by reason or result:

Psalm 34:9

⁹ Oh, fear the Lord, you his saints,
for those who fear him have no lack!

Many lines of synthetic parallelism simply advance or complete the thought, for example:

Psalm 23:6

⁶ Surely goodness and mercy shall follow me
   all the days of my life,
and I shall dwell in the house of the Lord
   forever.

Climactic Parallelism

Climactic parallelism in Hebrew poetry is a repetitive but advancing set of lines. Here is an example:

Psalm 29:1-2

¹ Ascribe to the Lord, O heavenly beings,
   ascribe to the Lord glory and strength.
² Ascribe to the Lord the glory due his name;
   worship the Lord in the splendor of holiness.

These types of poetic parallelism (synonymous, antithetical, synthetic and climactic) are literary styles which are straightforward and easily identified.

Chiasmic Parallelism

Chiasmic parallelism is a little more complex than the types of parallelism identified above. Chiasmic means crossing over or intersection. In rhetoric, chiasmus (Greek: χιάζω, chiázō) means to shape like the letter X. It is a figure of speech in which two or more clauses are related to each other. A chiasm (or chiasmus) is a writing style that uses a unique repetition pattern for clarification and emphasis. Often called the chiastic approach or the chiastic structure, this repetition form appears throughout the Bible. Chiasms are structured in a repeating A-B-C / C-B-A pattern. So a chiasm is a literary device in which a sequence of ideas is presented and then repeated in reverse order. The result is a mirror effect as the ideas are reflected back in a passage.

The structure of a chiasm may be expressed through a series of letters; each letter represents a new idea. For example, the structure ABBA refers to two ideas (A and B) repeated in reverse order (B and A). Often, a chiasm includes another idea in the middle of the repetition: ABXBA. In this structure, the two ideas (A and B) are repeated in reverse order, but a third idea is inserted before the repetition (X). By virtue of its position, the insertion is emphasized.

Some chiasms are quite simple. The common saying "When the going gets tough, the tough get going" is chiastic. The words "going" and "tough" are repeated, in reverse order, in the second half of the sentence. The structure is ABBA. Another example of a chiasm, also with the ABBA structure, is Benjamin Franklin's axiom "By failing to prepare, you are preparing to fail." It is a form of rhetoric that has an impact.

Many passages in the Bible exhibit chiastic structure. For example, Jesus' words in Mark 2:27 are in the form of a chiasm: "The Sabbath was made for man, not man for the Sabbath." Using the ABBA form, the words Sabbath and man are repeated in reverse order. Matthew 23:12 is another example, "Whoever exalts himself will be humbled, and whoever humbles himself will be exalted." A longer chiasm is found in Joel 3.

Joel 3:17-21

17 "So you shall know that I am the Lord your God,
   who dwells in Zion, my holy mountain.
And Jerusalem shall be holy,
   and strangers shall never again pass through it.

   18 "And in that day
the mountains shall drip sweet wine,
   and the hills shall flow with milk,
and all the streambeds of Judah
   shall flow with water;
and a fountain shall come forth from the house of the Lord
   and water the Valley of Shittim.

19 "Egypt shall become a desolation
   and Edom a desolate wilderness,
for the violence done to the people of Judah,
   because they have shed innocent blood in their land.
20 But Judah shall be inhabited forever,
   and Jerusalem to all generations.
21 I will avenge their blood,
   blood I have not avenged,
   for the Lord dwells in Zion."

This one has seven parts, diagrammed this way: ABCXCBA. The ideas presented in this prophecy follow this arrangement:

A - God dwells in Zion (verse 17a)

B - Jerusalem is holy (verse 17b)

C - Foreign invaders are banished (verse 17c)

X - The blessings of the Kingdom (verse 18)

C - Foreign enemies are destroyed (verse 19)

B - Jerusalem and Judah are preserved (verses 20–21a)

A - God dwells in Zion (verse 21b).

The central emphasis is the blessings of the Kingdom (X)

Here is another example:

Joshua 1:5-9

A - I will never leave you nor forsake you

B - Be strong and courageous ... be strong and very courageous

C - Be careful to obey all the law ... that you may be successful

D - Do not let this Book of the Law depart from your mouth

D - Mediate on it day and night

C - Be careful to do everything written in it ... you may be prosperous and successful

B - Be strong and courageous. Do not be terrified; do not be discouraged

A - for the Lord your God will be with you wherever you go.

The central emphasis here is

"Do not let this Book of the Law depart from your mouth.
Meditate on it day and night."

Simply put, a chiasm is a repetition of similar ideas in the reverse sequence ~ as in ABC – CBA above. So the chiastic structure is often used to add emphasis. The writers who inscribed their portions of the Hebrew and Greek Scriptures could not use the techniques that are available today on computers; such as emboldening, italicization, underlining, indenting, bulleting, or variations of font sizes, to draw the reader's attention to something. They used literary devices to structure arrangements of thoughts and words to accomplish this emphasis.

Jesus said "No one can serve two masters, for either he will hate the one and love the other, or he will be devoted to the one and despise the other. You cannot serve God and money." (Mt. 6:24) This statement is chiastic and could be represented thus:

A - No one can serve two masters.

B - Either he will hate the one and

C - love the other, or

C - he will be devoted to the one and

B - despise the other.

A - You cannot serve both God and Money

Note how the ideas A and A have similar themes, as do B and B and C and C. Therefore, this chiasm uses three themes:

1. serving one of two masters (God or money)

2. hating one of the masters

3. loving the other master

The theme in the middle portion of this text is called the center point ~ in this case, C and C is that center point. The portion in the center is usually the emphasis of the passage. The center point focuses on loving the right master. Serving God is good and proper. But love and devotion to him should be the emphasis or driving force. Some people serve the Lord but never love Him. The application is apparent ~ when we love God, serving him is a natural response. Therefore, this chiasm reveals that the emphasis is on loving God. The choice to serve him should be the outcome of that love. Seeing the chiasmic structure is the first step in understanding the intended emphasis.[45]

Figurative Language

The Bible is filled with figurative language. Its presence should cause the reader / interpreter to be even more careful in his treatment of the Bible. Care must be taken not to interpret literally that which was intended to be understood in a non-literal sense. Figurative language is also known as "trope." Trope is a word, phrase, expression, or image that is used in a figurative way, usually for rhetorical effect. Rhetoric is an eloquent way of speaking, relating to the skill of using language effectively and persuasively. Figurative language, of course, is not merely limited to the biblical writers. It has been universally discovered in every language and culture throughout human history. Figurative language provides depth, richness, and imagery in conversations. It enhances communication. In 1937, W. MacNeile Dixon (distinguished professor of English literature at the University of Glasgow) wrote:

> If I were asked what has been the most powerful force in the making of history...I should have answered...figurative expression. It is by imagination that men have lived; imagination rules all our lives. The human mind is not, as philosophers would have you think, a debating hall, but a picture gallery...Remove the metaphors [i.e., figurative expressions] from the Bible and its living spirit vanishes...The

---

[45] Not all chiasms have a center point of emphasis; for example, many of the A-B-B-A chiasms in Proverbs do not reveal their importance in this manner.

prophets, the poets, the leaders of men are all of them masters of imagery, and by imagery they capture the human soul.[46]

Figurative language is common. Note the following examples from both modern usage and ancient biblical usage:

Modern Usage

- "It's raining cats and dogs."

- "That argument doesn't hold any water."

- "He was so angry that he started to boil."

- "I was tickled to death."

- "When I heard the joke, I started to crack up."

- "Now, that's a heavy thought!"

Biblical Usage

- "Behold, the Lamb of God..." (Jn. 1:29)

- "Why will you still be struck down? Why will you continue to rebel? The whole head is sick, and the whole heart faint. From the sole of the foot even to the head, there is no soundness in it, but bruises and sores and raw wounds; they are not pressed out or bound up or softened with oil." (Isa. 1:5-6)

- I am weary with my moaning; every night I flood my bed with tears; I drench my couch with my weeping. (Ps. 6:6)

- "Truly, truly, I say to you, unless you eat the flesh of the Son of Man and drink his blood, you have no life in you. Whoever feeds on my flesh and drinks my blood has eternal life, and I will raise him up on the last day. For my flesh is true food, and my blood is true drink." (Jn. 6:53-55)

This has been interpreted in a literal way and distorts the truth. Jesus also said he was the door, but that is always understood as figurative language. When Jesus said, "You blind guides, straining out a gnat and swallowing a camel!" (Mt. 23:24) he was, of course, speaking figuratively.

---

[46] Cited in Roy Zuck, *Basic Bible Interpretation* (David C. Cook, 1991), 143.

What is the Purpose of Figurative Language?

Figures of speech add color or vividness to language and make abstract or intellectual ideas more concrete. Figurative language aids retention inasmuch as it makes indelible impressions on memory. Figures of speech abbreviate or condense an idea, and they can also encourage deeper reflection upon what is said. There are some basic types of figurative language used in literature, including the Bible. I list below some more figures of speech. These are not irrelevant in the interpretation of Scripture ~ in fact they can make a critical difference between interpretation and misinterpretation.

Simile

A simile is a comparison in which one thing is compared with another, usually with the expression "like" or "as." Terry defines it like this, "When a formal comparison is made between two different objects, so as to impress the mind with some resemblance or likeness, the figure is called a simile."[47] Here are some examples from Scripture:

> "For as the heavens are higher than the earth, so are my ways higher than your ways and my thoughts than your thoughts. For as the rain and the snow come down from heaven and do not return there but water the earth, making it bring forth and sprout, giving seed to the sower and bread to the eater, so shall my word be that goes out from my mouth: it shall not return to me empty, but it shall accomplish that which I purpose, and shall succeed in the thing for which I sent it."—Isaiah 55:9-11.

> "Is not my word like fire, declares the LORD, and like a hammer that breaks the rock in pieces?"—Jeremiah 23:29

> "Everyone then who hears these words of mine and does them will be like a wise man who built his house on the rock. And the rain fell, and the floods came, and the winds blew and beat on that house, but it did not fall, because it had been founded on the rock. And everyone who hears these words of mine and does not do them will be like a foolish man who built his house on the sand. And the rain fell, and the floods came, and the winds blew and beat against that house, and it fell, and great was the fall of it."—Matthew 7:24-27.

---

[47] Milton S. Terry, *Biblical Hermeneutics: a Treatise on the Interpretation of the Old and New Testaments* (Grand Rapids, Michigan: Zondervan, 1974), 254.

And when he came up out of the water, immediately he saw the heavens being torn open and the Spirit descending on him like a dove.'—Mark 1:10.

"All flesh is like grass and all its glory like the flower of grass. The grass withers, and the flower falls."—1 Peter 1:24.

Metaphor

A metaphor is a comparison in which one thing acts like or represents another, although the two are basically unalike.

"My people have been lost sheep. Their shepherds have led them astray, turning them away on the mountains. From mountain to hill they have gone. They have forgotten their fold."—Jeremiah 50:6.

"You are the salt of the earth, but if salt has lost its taste, how shall its saltiness be restored? It is no longer good for anything except to be thrown out and trampled under people's feet. You are the light of the world. A city set on a hill cannot be hidden."—Matthew 5:13-14.

"I am the bread of life."—John 6:48.

So Jesus again said to them, "Truly, truly, I say to you, I am the door of the sheep...I am the door. If anyone enters by me, he will be saved and will go in and out and find pasture."—John 10:7, 9.

Metonymy

Metonymy is the substituting of one word for another. For example, when we refer to a decision being made by the White House, we actually mean the president of the United States. We have simply substituted the residence of the president for the president himself.

"And if a house is divided against itself, that house will not be able to stand."—Mark 3:25.

Let marriage be held in honor among all, and let the marriage bed be undefiled, for God will judge the sexually immoral and adulterous.—Hebrews 13:4.

Hyperbole

Hyperbole is a deliberate exaggeration for the sake of effect. In hyperbole more is said than is literally meant. The purpose is to add emphasis or force.

Then Jerusalem and all Judea and all the region about the Jordan were going out to him.—Matthew 3:5.

"I am poured out like water, and all my bones are out of joint; my heart is like wax; it is melted within my breast."—Psalm 22:14.

Where are we going up? Our brothers have made our hearts melt, saying, "The people are greater and taller than we. The cities are great and fortified up to heaven. And besides, we have seen the sons of the Anakim there."—Deuteronomy 1:28.

Saul and Jonathan, beloved and lovely! In life and in death they were not divided; they were swifter than eagles; they were stronger than lions.—2 Samuel 1:23.

"I am weary with my moaning; every night I flood my bed with tears; I drench my couch with my weeping."—Psalm 6:6.

"If your right eye causes you to sin, tear it out and throw it away. For it is better that you lose one of your members than that your whole body be thrown into hell. And if your right hand causes you to sin, cut it off and throw it away. For it is better that you lose one of your members than that your whole body go into hell."—Matthew 5:29-30.

"Again I tell you, it is easier for a camel to go through the eye of a needle than for a rich person to enter the kingdom of God."—Matthew 19:24.

"You blind guides, straining out a gnat and swallowing a camel!"—Matthew 23:24.

Irony

Irony is a kind of ridicule expressed indirectly in the form of a compliment. Irony is often conveyed by the speaker's tone of voice (as in sarcasm) so that the hearers know immediately that irony is intended. Like sarcasm, it can be a remark that means the opposite of what it seems to say and is intended to mock or deride.

And David returned to bless his household. But Michal the daughter of Saul came out to meet David and said, "How the king of Israel honored himself today, uncovering himself today before the eyes of his servants' female servants, as one of the vulgar fellows shamelessly uncovers himself!"—2 Samuel 6:20.

And at noon Elijah mocked them, saying, "Cry aloud, for he is a god. Either he is musing, or he is relieving himself, or he is on a journey, or perhaps he is asleep and must be awakened."—1 Kings 18:27.

And he said to them, "You have a fine way of rejecting the commandment of God in order to establish your tradition!"—Mark 7:9.

According to Grant R. Osborne:

Irony is an important rhetorical device that consists of stating one thing while meaning the direct opposite. It is frequently employed in polemical contexts and is accompanied by sarcasm or ridicule, as in Michal's retort to David, 'How the King of Israel has distinguished himself today' (2 Samuel 6:20), with open contempt for his dancing before the ark...In such cases irony becomes biting sarcasm.[48]

Personification

This is the ascribing of human characteristics to inanimate objects. It could also be ascribing human actions or ideas to animals. For example, Proverbs 8 personifies wisdom.

The wilderness and the dry land shall be glad; the desert shall rejoice and blossom like the crocus.—Isaiah 35:1.

For you shall go out in joy and be led forth in peace; the mountains and the hills before you shall break forth into singing, and all the trees of the field shall clap their hands.—Isaiah 55:12.

Let the rivers clap their hands; let the hills sing for joy...—Psalm 98:8.

Anthropomorphism

It is giving human characteristics to something that is not human such as God or animals.

The eyes of the LORD are toward the righteous and his ears toward their cry. The face of the LORD is against those who do evil, to cut off the memory of them from the earth.—Psalm 34:15-16.

For the eyes of the LORD run to and fro throughout the whole earth, to give strong support to those whose heart is

---

[48] Grant R. Osborne, *The Hermeneutical Spiral: A Comprehensive Introduction to Biblical Interpretation* (IVP Academic; Revised and Expanded edition, 2007), 107.

blameless toward him. You have done foolishly in this, for from now on you will have wars.—2 Chronicles 16:9.

When I look at your heavens, the work of your fingers, the moon and the stars, which you have set in place.—Psalm 8:3.

Incline your ear to me; rescue me speedily!—Psalm 31:2.

Anthropopathism

This is the ascribing of human emotions to God.

And the LORD was sorry that he had made man on the earth, and it grieved him to his heart.—Genesis 6:6.

"Thus says the LORD of hosts: I am jealous for Zion with great jealousy, and I am jealous for her with great wrat.—Zechariah 8:2.

Both anthropomorphism and anthropopathism are critical in addressing the question, "does God change his mind."

> See Appendix 1: Does God Change His Mind?

Apostrophe

Apostrophe is addressing something absent as if it were present.

- Come now, you rich, weep and howl for the miseries that are coming upon you.—James 5:1.

- Death, where is your victory? O death, where is your sting?—1 Corinthians 15:55.

Synecdoche

Synecdoche (συνεκδοχή) is using part of something to represent the whole or the whole for the part. Synecdoche is a figure of speech used every day in English. For, example, describing a complete vehicle as "wheels" or referring to people by a particular body part, such as "head count" or "all hands on deck!" Many people say Holland, a region of the Netherlands, to refer to the entire country. There is a tendency to use a generic trademark, for example, "Coke" for any variety of cola or "Hoover" for vacuum cleaner. Some people would say "ivories" for a piano, as in, "The maestro sure knows how to tickle the ivories." One might say "he drank the cup," to refer to his drinking of the cup's contents. It is important that we become familiar with the figures of speech in Scripture.

Synecdoche is similar to Metonymy. In Metonymy, the exchange is made between two related nouns ~ the name of a person, place or thing (such as "Whitehouse" for "president"). In Synecdoche, the exchange is made between two associated ideas.

There are many examples in the Bible, such as, "...And all the people gathered around Jeremiah in the house of the LORD." (Jer. 26:9b). Not "everyone" did, as is clear from the context, but a large number did. Referring to John the Baptist Matthew says, "Then Jerusalem and all Judea and all the region about the Jordan were going out to him." (Mt. 3:5).

Not "all" the people were going, but a large number were. Synecdoche gives us a feel for the large numbers of people that responded to John the Baptist. Another example is, "So Hazael went to meet him [Elisha], and took a present with him, all kinds of goods of Damascus, forty camel loads..." (2 Kings 8:9a). The Hebrew text reads that Hazael took "every good thing of Damascus" to Elisha. This, of course, is impossible. This is a Synecdoche, the whole for a part. The phrase "Hazael took every kind of good thing" is interesting. It is an example of the English versions (such as the ESV) interpreting rather than translating. That does not give the English reader the chance to see the Synecdoche.

The King James Version (KJV) of James 2:15a says, "If a brother or sister be naked..." but the English Standard Version (ESV) says, "If a brother or sister is poorly clothed" ~ "naked" is Synecdoche for "poorly clothed." This is a common Synecdoche in the Bible.

Again, the KJV says, "Therefore that disciple whom Jesus loved saith unto Peter, It is the Lord. Now when Simon Peter heard that it was the Lord, he girt his fisher's coat unto him, (for he was naked,) and did cast himself into the sea." (Jn. 21:7).[49] But would he have worked that way? Unlikely, especially since fishing boats on the Sea of Tiberias could easily be seen from shore. The ESV says, "he put on his outer garment, for he was stripped for work, and threw himself into the sea." In the Greek this verse reads:

λέγει οὖν ὁ μαθητὴς ἐκεῖνος ὃν ἠγάπα ὁ Ἰησοῦς τῷ Πέτρῳ· Ὁ κύριός ἐστιν. Σίμων οὖν Πέτρος, ἀκούσας ὅτι ὁ κύριός ἐστιν, τὸν ἐπενδύτην διεζώσατο, ἦν γὰρ γυμνός, καὶ ἔβαλεν ἑαυτὸν εἰς τὴν θάλασσαν·

---

[49] Notice the gospel formula where the author does not mention himself directly. The same is true of Mark concerning the disciple that fled naked. That is why we assume it was Mark himself.

Putting on a coat is a peculiar way to prepare for a swim, especially in hasty preparation. Working in the nude also seems to defy Jewish sensibilities. Scholarship (BDAG ~ the common abbreviation Bauer and Danker) is clear that γυμνός does not necessarily mean completely naked (and this is variously reflected in more recent translations).[50] It pertains to being inadequately clothed...without an outer garment, without which a decent person did not appear in public. It makes sense that Peter might be working in his undergarments and feel inadequately clothed to meet the Lord. However, swimming in a coat just seems like a bad idea. The New English Translation (NET) of the Bible has an interesting take on it, quoting the footnote 2 on v. 7:

> The Greek verb used (διαζώννυμι, diazwnnumi) does not necessarily mean putting clothing on, but rather tying the clothing around oneself (the same verb is used in 13:4-5 of Jesus tying the towel around himself). The statement that Peter was "naked" could just as well mean that he was naked underneath the outer garment, and thus could not take it off before jumping into the water. But he did pause to tuck it up and tie it with the girdle before jumping in, to allow himself more freedom of movement. Thus the clause that states Peter was naked is explanatory (note the use of for), explaining why Peter girded up his outer garment rather than taking it off — he had nothing on underneath it and so could not remove it.

The psalmist says, "For I will not trust in my bow..." (Ps. 44:6a) - "bow" is Synecdoche for all weapons. The point is that David will not trust his weapons, he will trust his God. If the verse had said "I will not trust in my human resources" we are left with no clear picture in our minds. By saying "bow," we can picture David holding a bow but not trusting it to deliver him. The language is vivid.

Genesis says, "By the sweat of your face you shall eat bread, till you return to the ground" (Gen. 3:19a) - "bread" speaks of all kinds of food. Bread is used as the general term for food many times in the Bible. The phrase "break bread" means to eat a meal. The Lord's Prayer says "Give us this day our daily bread," which refers to food in a general sense. The apostle Paul wrote, "For we do not wrestle against flesh and blood." (Eph. 6:12a) In this case, "flesh and blood" means "people." The verse could have been written in a simple literal way, using "people" instead of "flesh and blood" but the use of the synecdoche more powerfully contrasts people with demons, who are not flesh and blood.

---

[50] Walter Bauer (Author), Frederick William Danker (Editor) *A Greek-English Lexicon of the New Testament and Other Early Christian Literature*, (3rd edition, University of Chicago Press, 2001).

Interpretation of Parables

What exactly is a parable? A parable uses comparisons, often in the form of a story. The stories help us remember the point that is being made. This is particularly so in an oral culture, but still relevant in a culture where the written word is more common. They also serve to hide the truths being taught from those who are not seriously seeking and who have hardened their hearts.—Matthew 13:10-15.

Parables convict those who know the truth but who are not living according to that truth ~ this is evident in Nathan's confrontation of King David's adultery. The function of parables is to bring forth a response from the hearer. In interpreting parables, identify the audience and you will gain insight into the point(s) being made. According to Zuck:

> A parable is a form of figurative language involving comparisons. But rather than using a single word or phrase to make the comparison or analogy, as in a simile, metaphor, or hypocatastasis, a parable is an extended analogy in story form. A parable is a true-to-life story to illustrate or illumine a truth. It is true to life though it may not have actually occurred in all the details as the story is presented. Historic events may serve as illustrations; but parables are special stories, not necessarily historic events, that are told to teach a particular truth. Since parables are true to life, they differ from allegories and fables...The word 'parable' comes from the Greek *para* ('beside or alongside') and *ballein* ('to throw'). Thus the story is thrown alongside the truth to illustrate the truth."[51]

Why did Jesus Speak in Parables?

Jesus spoke in parables in order to reveal spiritual truth to his disciples and to conceal it from those whose hearts were hardened to the message of the kingdom. Jesus explained the purpose of the parables thus:

> Then the disciples came and said to him, "Why do you speak to them in parables?" And he answered them, "To you it has been given to know the secrets of the kingdom of heaven, but to them, it has not been given. For to the one who has, more will be given, and he will have an abundance, but from the one who has not, even what he has will be taken away. This is why I speak to them in parables because seeing they do not see, and hearing they do not hear, nor do they understand. Indeed, in their case, the prophecy of Isaiah is fulfilled that says:

---

[51] Roy B. Zuck, *Basic Bible Interpretation*, (David C. Cook, 1991), 194.

"'You will indeed hear but never understand, and you will indeed see but never perceive. For this people's heart has grown dull, and with their ears they can barely hear, and their eyes they have closed, lest they should see with their eyes and hear with their ears and understand with their heart and turn, and I would heal them.' But blessed are your eyes, for they see, and your ears, for they hear. For truly, I say to you, many prophets and righteous people longed to see what you see, and did not see it, and to hear what you hear, and did not hear it.—Matthew 13:10-17.

Not all the parables were explained. But Jesus explained the Parable of the Sower:

"Hear then the parable of the sower: When anyone hears the word of the kingdom and does not understand it, the evil one comes and snatches away what has been sown in his heart. This is what was sown along the path. As for what was sown on rocky ground, this is the one who hears the word and immediately receives it with joy, yet he has no root in himself, but endures for a while, and when tribulation or persecution arises on account of the word, immediately he falls away. As for what was sown among thorns, this is the one who hears the word, but the cares of the world and the deceitfulness of riches choke the word, and it proves unfruitful. As for what was sown on good soil, this is the one who hears the word and understands it. He indeed bears fruit and yields, in one case a hundredfold, in another sixty, and in another thirty."—Matthew 13:18-23.

Parables helped to illustrate truth as well as spark interest. People relate to a good story. By using parables Jesus was able to capture and sustain the interest of the crowds. In an oral culture (primarily) stories are easy to listen to and easier to remember than a didactic monologue. Parables encouraged listeners to think deeply about what Jesus said. Terry notes:

The general design of parables, as of all other kinds of figurative language, is to embellish and set forth ideas and moral truths in attractive and impressive forms. Many a moral lesson, if spoken in naked, literal style, is soon forgotten; but, clothed in parabolic dress, it arouses attention, and fastens itself in the memory. Many rebukes and pungent warnings may be couched in a parable, and thereby give less offence, and yet work better effects than open plainness of speech could do. Nathan's parable (in 2 Samuel 12:1-4) prepared the heart of David to receive with profit the keen reproof he was about to administer...It is easy, also, to see that a parable may enshrine a profound truth or mystery which the hearers may not at first apprehend, but which, because of its striking or memorable form, abides more firmly in the mind, and so abiding, yields at length its deep and precious meaning.[52]

Parables use figurative language to make truths more attractive and memorable. Moral lessons in didactic style are soon forgotten. Parables can contain stern rebukes and dire warnings. In parable form, they are less offensive. Yet they are more effective than plain speech. Consider the following parable about Nathan rebuking David:

> And the LORD sent Nathan to David. He came to him and said to him, "There were two men in a certain city, the one rich and the other poor. The rich man had very many flocks and herds, but the poor man had nothing but one little ewe lamb, which he had bought. And he brought it up, and it grew up with him and with his children. It used to eat of his morsel and drink from his cup and lie in his arms, and it was like a daughter to him. Now there came a traveler to the rich man, and he was unwilling to take one of his own flock or herd to prepare for the guest who had come to him, but he took the poor man's lamb and prepared it for the man who had come to him." Then David's anger was greatly kindled against the man, and he said to Nathan, "As the LORD lives, the man who has done this deserves to die, and he shall restore the lamb fourfold, because he did this thing, and because he had no pity." Nathan said to David, "You are the man!"—2 Samuel 12:1-7.

Nathan's parable (vs.1-4) prepared the heart of David to receive the rebuke.

A parable may contain a profound truth which the hearers may not immediately understand. Parables linger in the mind. They eventually yield their deep and precious meaning.

Classification of Parables

Jesus told many parables, which may generally be classified as follows:[53]

---

[52] Milton S. Terry, *Biblical Hermeneutics: a Treatise on the Interpretation of the Old and New Testaments*, (Grand Rapids, Michigan: Zondervan, 1974), 277-8.

[53] There may be some overlap with categories.

Seed parables ~ e.g., the Sower (Mt. 13:3-8); the Weeds (Mt. 13:24-30); the Mustard Seed (Mt. 13:31-32).

Nature parables ~ e.g. the Fishing Net (Mt. 13:47-50); the Barren Fig Tree (Lk. 13:6-9); the Lost Sheep (Lk. 15:4-7).

Servant parables ~ e.g., the Two Servants (Mt. 24:45-51); the Unforgiving Servant (Mt. 18:23-35); the Shrewd Manager (Lk. 16:1-9); the Servant's Reward (Lk. 17:7-10).

Father parables ~ e.g., the Two Sons (Mt. 21:28-32); the Prodigal Son (Lk. 15:11-32).

King parables ~ e.g., the Wedding Banquet (Mt. 22:1-14); the King's Rash War (Lk. 14:31-33).

Money or treasure parables ~ e.g., the Hidden Treasure (Mt. 13:44); the Talents (Mt. 25:14-30); the Shrewd Manager (Lk. 16:1-9); the Lost Coin (Lk. 15:8-10).

Harvest parables ~ e.g., the Wicked Vinegrowers (Mt 21:33-46); the Seed Growing Secretly (Mk. 4:26-29).

Women parables ~ e.g., the Ten Virgins (Mt. 25:1-13); The Persistent Widow (Lk. 18:1-8).

Social or domestic parables ~ e.g., the Great Banquet (Lk. 14:15-24); the Doorkeeper (Mt. 13:34-37); the Good Samaritan (Lk. 10:25-37).

Compassion parables ~ e.g., the Lost Sheep (Lk. 15:4-7); the Prodigal Son (Lk. 15:11-32); the Good Samaritan (Lk. 10:25-37).

Kingdom parables ~ e.g., the Mustard Seed (Mt. 13:31-32); the Pearl of Great Price (Mt. 13:45-46); the Net (Mt. 13:47-52); the Wedding Banquet (Mt. 22:1-14).

Judgment parables ~ e.g., the Rich Man and Lazarus (Lk. 16:19-31); the Wicked Vinegrowers or Farmers (Mt. 21:33-41).

How Should We Approach Parables and their Interpretation?

First, recognize the Christological nature of Jesus' parables. When Jesus employed parables, he was not merely attempting to illustrate a moral truth. Many rabbis did this during the first century. Jesus was illustrating some spiritual truth about himself. We must ask ourselves: how does this parable relate to Christ? This is what makes Jesus unique from others. His parables portrayed spiritual and heavenly realities. However, many of them also pointed directly to his person.

Second, another important principle is the kingdom principle. One of the major themes that Jesus frequently addressed was the kingdom of God. He talked about its nature, inhabitants, nearness, and its consummation. By "consummation" we mean bringing the kingdom to a final and satisfying completion. We must also ask ourselves, what does it say about the kingdom of God? What is the central lesson in the kingdom narrative?

Third, determine the one central truth which the parable is attempting to teach. According to C. H. Dodd, "The typical parable presents one single point of comparison. The details are not intended to have independent significance."[54] Do not try to hunt for distinct meanings in every detail within a parable. To do so would turn the story into an allegory ~ in an allegory the characters and events are understood as representing other things. As such they are symbolic and express a deeper, often spiritual, moral, or political meaning. So a parable is not an allegory! One well-known example of violating this principle is Augustine's allegorizing of the *Parable of the Good Samaritan*. Here is the parable from the Gospel of Luke:

> And behold, a lawyer stood up to put him to the test, saying, "Teacher, what shall I do to inherit eternal life?" He said to him, "What is written in the Law? How do you read it?" And he answered, "You shall love the Lord your God with all your heart and with all your soul and with all your strength and with all your mind, and your neighbor as yourself." And he said to him, "You have answered correctly; do this, and you will live." But he, desiring to justify himself, said to Jesus, "And who is my neighbor?" Jesus replied, "A man was going down from Jerusalem to Jericho, and he fell among robbers, who stripped him and beat him and departed, leaving him half dead. Now by chance a priest was going down that road, and when he saw him, he passed by on the other side. So likewise a Levite, when he came to the place and saw him, passed by on the other side. But a Samaritan, as he journeyed, came to where he was, and when he saw him, he had compassion. He went to him and bound up his wounds, pouring on oil and wine. Then he set him on his own animal and brought him to an inn and took care of him. And the next day he took out two denarii and gave them to the innkeeper, saying, 'Take care of him, and whatever more you spend, I will repay you when I come back.' Which of these three, do you think, proved to be a neighbor to

---

[54] C. H. Dodd, *The Parables of the Kingdom*, (Charles Scribner's Sons; Revised edition, 1961), 18.

the man who fell among the robbers?" He said, "The one who showed him mercy." And Jesus said to him, "You go, and do likewise."—Luke. 10:25-37).[55]

Here is Augustine's allegorical interpretation of that parable:

A certain man went down from Jerusalem to Jericho; Adam himself is meant; Jerusalem is the heavenly city of peace, from whose blessedness Adam fell; Jericho means the moon, and signifies our mortality, because it is born, waxes, wanes, and dies. Thieves are the devil and his angels. Who stripped him, namely; of his immortality; and beat him, by persuading him to sin; and left him half-dead, because in so far as man can understand and know God, he lives, but in so far as he is wasted and oppressed by sin, he is dead; he is therefore called half-dead. The priest and the Levite, who saw him and passed by, signify the priesthood and ministry of the Old Testament which could profit nothing for salvation. Samaritan means Guardian, and therefore the Lord Himself is signified by this name. The binding of the wounds is the restraint of sin. Oil is the comfort of good hope; wine the exhortation to work with fervent spirit. The beast is the flesh in which He deigned to come to us. The being set upon the beast is belief in the incarnation of Christ. The inn is the Church, where travelers returning to their heavenly country are refreshed after pilgrimage. The morrow is after the resurrection of the Lord. The two pence are either the two precepts of love, or the promise of this life and of that which is to come. The innkeeper is the Apostle (Paul). The supererogatory payment is either his counsel of celibacy, or the fact that he worked with his own hands lest he should be a burden to any of the weaker brethren when the Gospel was new, though it was lawful for him "to live by the gospel."[56]

This kind of absurd interpretation is to be avoided. There has been, historically, a tendency for preachers to *spiritualize* what was intended to *radicalize* social structures, thus avoiding the true spiritual implications of the text.

---

[55] The difference between a priest and a Levite in this parable is that all priests were Levites but not all Levites were priests.

[56] Augustine, *Quaestiones Evangeliorum*, II, 19 –slightly abridged as cited in C.H. Dodd, *The Parables of the Kingdom* (New York: Scribners, 1961), 1-2.

Fourth, determine how much of the parable is actually interpreted by Jesus himself. For instance, the *Parable of the Sower* in Matthew 13:3-8 is interpreted in verses 18-23.

Fifth, concerning the parable's meaning, we should look for clues within the immediate and surrounding context. In some instances, the meaning will become obvious by simply examining the context. There we might find what prompted the parable in the first place.

Sixth, compare the parable with any possible Old Testament association. Both Jesus and his listeners were familiar with much of the Old Testament. So, be alert to any possible Old Testament references in the parables ~ that is, references to such things as vineyards, fig trees, harvests, and feasts.

Seventh, it is wise not to build entire doctrinal systems from parables. Certainly, parables contain doctrine, but careful interpretation is necessary. Any doctrine which is gleaned from a parable ought to accord with the rest of the New Testament. If proper cautions are followed, parables may be used to illustrate doctrine and to teach practical lessons.

CHAPTER 7 Prophecy

Many people assume that the prophet's ministry was primarily concerned with predicting future events. However, the Old Testament reveals that prophetic revelation was much broader than this. There is certainly a *foretelling* of future events, but there is also a *forth-telling* of the revealed mind and heart of God. This is a very important dimension of prophecy. Thus, prophecy was not always futuristic. Prophecy spoke into the contemporary context. So we can speak today of preaching prophetically. This can be done in two ways. First, we can preach eschatologically. Scripture speaks of future events, which are yet to happen. One such event is the Lord's second coming. Second, we can preach the revealed mind of God for our generation. This is not to say that preaching and prophecy are the same things. The prophet was understood as a forth-teller of God's message. He frequently declared God's message of judgment on an unrepentant people. His message related to people who lived at the time the message was spoken.

The prophet ministered *in* and *to* the historical period in which he lived, but he was also a foreteller of future events. There were predictive elements in the prophet's oracles. They often spoke of the Messiah and his kingdom. Berkhof defines prophecy in the following manner, "Prophecy may simply be defined as the proclamation of that which God revealed."[57]

In prophecy, the central or primary meaning is significant. Focus on this rather than the relatively minor details in the prophet's message. This is similar to how we interpret parables. We must try to avoid deriving obscure meanings from the various details of the prophecy. We should fix our attention on the central thrust of the prophet's discourse. For example, in Isaiah 11:6-9 the prophet describes the universal peace which shall exist during the messianic age. We see this in terms of wild animals living peaceably with the rest of creation. Yet, later in Isaiah 35:8-10, this same period is described as having no wild animals present. Is there a contradiction? Not at all! The metaphorical details may change in each respective narrative. However, the central message of universal peace in the messianic age remains the same. Our focus must be on the primary intended meaning and not upon the details *per se*.

Let me give another example. Many have interpreted Ezekiel chapters 40-48 as describing the future millennial temple and its worship. An elaborate description is given of the temple and its measurements. This

---

[57] Louis Berkhof, *Principles of Biblical Interpretation* (Grand Rapids, Michigan: Baker Book House, 1950), 148.

has led many to interpret these chapters literally. These chapters give a detailed description of the various sacrifices that are to be offered at the temple (45:15-20). In their thinking, a literal and physical temple will be rebuilt in Jerusalem during the millennial age. Nevertheless, they also think there will be a sacrificial system without expiatory value ~ although the animal sacrifices are alleged to be memorial sacrifices. However, the Old Covenant sacrificial system has been abolished with the coming of Christ. It would be retrogressive to return to such types and shadows. What would be the point of all this when the Lord Jesus has already given us a memorial of his death in the Lord's Supper?

We must not fail to understand the figurative element in prophecy. We must focus on the central meaning that the prophet is attempting to convey. Some have misunderstood these important chapters. They have erected a theology which contradicts the fuller revelation of God found in the New Testament. Ezekiel is simply describing the glorious worship of God's people in the age to come. He is describing it in terms and ideas, which the Jews of that period would have understood. As Anthony Hoekema has written:

> Ezekiel gives no indication in these chapters that he is describing something which is to happen during a millennium preceding the final state. An interpretation of these chapters which is in agreement with New Testament teaching, and which avoids the absurdity of positing the need for memorial sacrifices in the millennium, understands Ezekiel to be describing here the glorious future of the people of God in the age to come in terms which the Jews of that day would understand. Since their worship previous to their captivity had been centered in the Jerusalem temple, it is understandable that Ezekiel describes their future blessedness by picturing a temple and its sacrifices. The details about temple and sacrifices are to be understood not literally but figuratively...What we have in Ezekiel 40 to 48, therefore, is not a description of the millennium but a picture of the final state on the new earth, in terms of the religious symbolism with which Ezekiel and his readers were familiar.[58]

Figurative Elements of Prophecy

We need to recognize the figurative or non-literal elements of prophecy. Much of the prophetic portions of Scripture are presented in figurative language. They are rich in symbolism, and dramatic imagery. The reason for this is often to emphasize the gravity and imminence of

---

[58] Anthony Hoekema, *The Bible and the Future*, (Wm. B. Eerdmans, 1994), 204-5.

God's judgment. Such picturesque language was familiar to the prophet's audience. They would have understood it as a way of describing God's intervention in history. Isaiah uses cosmic imagery:

> Behold, the day of the LORD comes, cruel, with wrath and fierce anger, to make the land a desolation and to destroy its sinners from it. For the stars of the heavens and their constellations will not give their light; the sun will be dark at its rising, and the moon will not shed its light. I will punish the world for its evil, and the wicked for their iniquity; I will put an end to the pomp of the arrogant, and lay low the pompous pride of the ruthless.—Isaiah 13:9-11.

To many, this would appear to describe the end of the world. But the passage is about God's judgment upon the Babylonian empire approximately six-hundred years before the birth of Christ. As the opening verse of that chapter will attest, "The oracle concerning Babylon, which Isaiah the son of Amoz saw." (Isa. 13:1). This is confirmed later in the chapter, "...Babylon, the glory of kingdoms, the splendor, and pomp of the Chaldeans, will be like Sodom and Gomorrah when God overthrew them."—Isaiah 13:19.

In Acts 2:14-21, Peter interprets the prophecy and cosmic imagery of Joel 2:28-32 as having its fulfillment on the day of Pentecost. The cosmic signs (expressed by Joel) did not literally occur at Pentecost. But what the author willed to convey by those signs did. Some say that Joel's prophecy was only partially fulfilled at Pentecost. They say that its final fulfillment will take place when Christ returns. However, as Robert H. Stein notes, this interpretation does not satisfy the words of Peter:

> There have been attempts to deny that the prophecy of Joel 2:28-32 was fulfilled at Pentecost. Usually this is due to a misunderstanding of the figurative nature of this cosmic terminology. Some have suggested that Luke and Peter believed that Pentecost was 'kind of like' what Joel prophesied but not its actual fulfillment. Such a manipulative interpretation of this passage of Acts, however, is impossible in light of Peter's words in Acts 2:16: 'this is what was spoken by the prophet Joel.' Furthermore such interpretive gymnastics are unnecessary when we are willing to accept what the author meant by the use of such terminology. We need only note other passages to see how widespread the use of such cosmic terminology is in the Bible (Isaiah 24:23; Jeremiah 4:28; 13:16; 15:9; Ezekiel 32:7-8; Joel 2:10,31; 3:15; Amos 8:9; Habakkuk 3:11; Matthew 24:29; Mark 13:24-25; Luke 21:25; Revelation 6:12). Attempts to see Mark 15:33; Matthew 27:45; Luke 23:44-45 as the fulfillment

of this prophecy err. They do not explain the signs of Acts 2:19 and most of 2:20. Second, and more important, they err because Peter and Luke associated the fulfillment of these signs with what is happening then and there on the day of Pentecost.[59]

Does the prophecy have its fulfillment in the historical period in which they were announced? This should be asked first when considering a prophetic passage. By doing so, we will avoid the common abuse of many preachers who engage in a sort of "newspaper exegesis" whereby they wrongly interpret prophetic passages. Because such passages have a historical context they refer to events and fulfillment in the life of Israel and should not be automatically projected to a distant future. Osborne warns us against such mistaken notions:

> I would add a fifth type of erroneous preaching, the 'newspaper' approach of many so-called prophecy preachers today. This school assumes that the prophecies were not meant for the ancient setting but rather for the modern setting. Amazingly, that setting is often post-1948 (after Israel became a nation) America. Such preachers ignore the fact that God chose all the symbols and passages to speak to Israel and that modern people must understand them in their ancient context before applying them today...'Newspaper' preachers instead take prophetic passages out of context and twist them to fit the modern situation. This is dangerous for it too easily leads to a subjective 'eisegesis' (reading meaning into a text), which does anything one wants to the Scriptural text...Many today leap too quickly into a futuristic interpretation of passages that were more likely meant to speak to the author's own day.[60]

Many prophetic passages were meant to speak to the author's own day.

Recognize the Non-Systematic Character of Prophecy

The prophetic portions of Scripture are not organized as systematically as one might suppose or wish. Ramm points out:

---

[59] Robert H. Stein, *A Basic Guide to Interpreting the Bible: Playing by the Rules* (Baker Academic; 2 edition, 2011), 93.

[60] Grant R. Osborne, *The Hermeneutical Spiral: A Comprehensive Introduction to Biblical Interpretation* (Second edition. Downers Grove, Ill.: InterVarsity Press, 2006), 217-8.

The future may appear present, or nearby, or indefinitely remote. Widely separated events on the actual calendar of history may appear together in the prophetic sequence. The Jewish scholars unable to decipher pictures of Messianic suffering and Messianic glory were not properly prepared for the advent of the humiliation of our Lord. Only in the pages of the New Testament are these two pictures properly related in terms of two advents of the Messiah (cf. 1 Peter 1:10-12 and Hebrews 9:28).[61]

Direct Prediction and Fulfilment

Specific verses from the Old Testament were understood as directly predicting the person and work of Christ (for example, Isa. 53; Micah 5:2 ~ Mt. 2:4-6). See Acts 8: 26-40 Philip and the Ethiopian eunuch and note v. 35. In such instances, there is a one-to-one correspondence between an Old Testament prediction and its New Testament fulfillment.

Therefore, the prophet discloses God's will and words to the people (forth-telling). This word may be a prediction that refers to future events (foretelling). Prophecy related very much to the present contemporary realities of the time when they were issued. In that sense, they reveal the meaning of the present from a true spiritual perspective. Prophecy may give instruction, offer comfort, exhortation, or confrontation. Prophets spoke God's words, not their own. Most of their future predictions are now past. They tell the story of and the prophet's interaction with God and people surrounding them.

Types of Prophecy

There are different types of prophecy, which may be categorized as follows:

- Disaster ~ Isa.30:15-17

- Salvation ~ Jer.28:2-4

- Woe speech ~ Mic.2:1-5

- Prophetic dirge (over Israel) ~ Amos 5:1-3

- Prophetic hymn ~ Amos 4:13

- Prophetic liturgy ~ Jer.14:1-3, 7, 9-22

---

[61] Bernard Ramm, *Protestant Biblical Interpretation: A Textbook of Hermeneutics*, (3rd edition, Grand Rapids, Mich.: Baker Book House, 1970), 249.

- Prophetic disputation ~ Amos 3:3-8

- Prophetic lawsuit ~ Isa.3:13-36

- Prophecy against foreign nations

- Prophetic vision ~ reports include things that they saw (Isa. 6)

- Prophetic narratives relate how God called and commissioned the prophets

How to Interpret Prophecy

As always, historical-cultural analysis is crucially important. Bible dictionaries and encyclopedias are essential tools. Commentaries are also important. We must also see how people in the Bible understood the language that was used. Did they understand the language figuratively or literally? As you read through the prophets, think oracles rather than chapters or paragraphs. What was the oracle of God on any one particular occasion?

Can a prophecy have more than one meaning? Yes. There can be multiple fulfillment (see Caiaphas' prophecy in Jn. 11:50). The prophets must have understood what they said and meant at one level. However, they may not have understood the full implications of their words.

Literal Versus Symbolic

Should we understand that prophecies used the language of the day but refer to modern realities? For example, could swords and horses in the text actually refer to modern guns and tanks? How much should be interpreted literally and how much symbolically or spiritually? The prophets often express poetically what will happen. Will lions lying down with lambs be literally true during a millennium or is this poetic for the peace that will exist during the eternal state?

Is the prophecy meant to be understood universally or is it limited? How conditional are prophecies? Jonah's prophecy of the destruction of Nineveh was conditional, but this was not stated by him. Do we understand that God changed his mind about certain prophecies?

With prophecy, there can be a literal and/or figurative fulfillment.

CHAPTER 8 New Testament uses of the Old Testament

There are approximately three hundred instances where the New Testament quotes from the Old Testament. The New Testament revelation of Christ fulfills the Old Testament promises and types. There is great continuity between the two Testaments. There is also discontinuity.[62] Regarding prophecies, some are introductory formulas (e.g., "As it is written"). Some are exact quotes. Others are summaries or loose paraphrases of Old Testament passages.

Problems may arise when New Testament writers fail to quote verbatim from the Hebrew Bible or when they discover meanings from Old Testament passages, which seem to run counter to its original intended meaning. The question arises, therefore, "does the New Testament distort the Old Testament? Were the apostles of Christ taking undue liberty by reinterpreting certain Old Testament passages? Can we legitimately adhere to the doctrine of inerrancy in light of such apparent abuses of the Old Testament? This is not a simple matter to resolve. But there are answers to such questions. These answers vindicate the doctrine of inerrancy. Such answers prove that the New Testament writers did not abuse the Old Testament Scriptures.

Exact, verbatim quotations were not as common in the Greco-Roman world of the first century A.D. as in our modern era of the twenty-first century. Usually, a summary or paraphrase was sufficient to make one's point. This is especially true in the case of the ancient Rabbis who quoted the Old Testament extensively. They did not always quote with precision. The intended meaning was the important thing. Dynamic equivalency rather than verbatim interpretation was the order of the day. To hold the New Testament writers to a level of precision, which was rarely practiced in their time, is unfair. In fact, there are several instances when later portions of the Old Testament quote from earlier ones without adhering to an exact verbal procedure.

Gospel writers can cite Old Testament verses and apply them to Jesus. Sometimes the phrase "Thus it was fulfilled" is used. The majority of New Testament uses of the Bible follow a non-literal interpretation. New Testament scholar, Donald A. Hagner, makes this clear:

> However, such clear predictive prophecy and fulfillment is seldom found in the New Testament; it is the exception rather

---

[62] See section that deals with the three dimensions of Law: moral, judicial and ceremonial.

than the rule. Instead...the New Testament writers looked for the meaning of the Old Testament as contained in its *Sensus Plenior* (full meaning). In so doing, they found varied correspondences, analogies, and suggestive similarities – some more substantial, some less substantial – but all based on the underlying presuppositions of the sovereignty of God in the affairs of history; the unique character of the Scriptures as divinely inspired; and the identity of Jesus as the *telos*, or goal, of the history of salvation.[63]

The same points are made by S. Lewis Johnson, Jr. who writes:

It is a common misconception of casual Bible readers that when the New Testament states that a text from the Old Testament is fulfilled in the New, the use of the Old Testament text is that of precise predictive fulfillment. Thus readers are puzzled when they discover from a careful reading of the Old Testament that the Old Testament passage does not seem to speak precisely of what the New Testament seems to suggest. They fail to bear in mind the philosophy of the biblical authors. The writers of Scripture believed that God controlled history. Therefore, history of all kinds, especially the sacred record, spoke ultimately of the activities of the triune God. They did not think it necessary to define the precise kind of fulfillment found in New Testament texts, for it was God who controlled the prophets who wrote direct predictive prophecy and the other authors of Scripture who wrote of people, events, and institutions as types or foreshadowings of the future. Thus both kinds of material were fulfilled in the New Testament, although in a slightly different way.[64]

The New Testament employs the Old Testament in a variety of ways. It does so to demonstrate that, in Jesus, the biblical prophecies, types, and shadows have all found their divinely appointed fulfillment.

Typology

Typology is a method of biblical interpretation. It is when an element found in the Old Testament is seen to prefigure one found in the

---

[63] Donald A. Hagner, "The Old Testament in the New Testament," *Interpreting the Word of God*, (eds. Samuel J. Schultz & Morris A. Inch, Chicago: Moody Press, 1976), 103.

NOTE: Telos (Greek τέλος for "end," "purpose," or "goal").

[64] S. Lewis Johnson, *The Old Testament in the New: An Argument for Biblical Inspiration Contemporary Evangelical Perspectives*, (Zondervan, 1980), 76.

New Testament. The initial one is called the type, and the fulfillment is designated the antitype. Either type or antitype may be a person, thing, or event. Often the type is messianic and frequently related to the idea of salvation. The use of biblical typology enjoyed greater popularity in previous centuries. It is by no means ignored as a principle of hermeneutics today. Typological interpretation of the Old Testament is based on the fundamental theological unity of the two Testaments. Thus something in the Old shadows or prefigures something in the New. The study of types, particularly, types of Christ, is motivated by a number of factors related to New Testament use of the Old Testament.

Firstly, the authors of various New Testament books use the Old Testament as a source of pictures pointing forward to Jesus. Among the most obvious passages is 1 Cor. 10:1–6, Gal. 4:21-31 and the letter to the Hebrews. From 1 Corinthians, we find Paul using the desert wanderings as typological of the Christian life. The author of Hebrews is concerned to write explaining how the Old Testament points forward to Jesus. In so doing, he draws heavily on Moses the man, as well as the Mosaic Law, with its sacrifices and Temple rituals.

Classification of Types

There are various types presented in the Old Testament. Chief among these are the historical, legal and the prophetic types. Firstly, historical types are people in the Old Testament who are frequently seen to be types of Christ. Moses, for instance, led God's people out of slavery in Egypt. He is clearly a type for the Messiah because Jesus leads his people out of the slavery of sin. A host of Old Testament characters can be seen, in this manner, to act as types of Christ. Secondly, there are legal types. Within the Law of Moses, many sacrifices, offerings and rituals were prescribed by God as the worship to be given by Israel. These sacrifices pointed forward to the one Sacrifice to be offered on the Cross for the sins of all who would repent and trust Jesus by faith. Thirdly, there are prophetic types. Imagery occurs frequently in the prophetic books and other prophecies contained in Scripture. Genesis 3:15 For instance, contains the gospel, "I will put enmity between you and the woman, and between your offspring and her offspring; he shall bruise your head, and you shall bruise his heel." The Seed of the woman (Jesus) would crush the head of the serpent (Satan) once and for all on the cross at Calvary. God spoke these words to Adam and Eve in the Garden of Eden before their expulsion. This verse has prophetic and messianic fulfillment in Christ. It is for this reason that this verse is called the *protoevangelium* (first gospel).

Survey of Perspectives on Typology

The historical development of perspectives regarding typology is important for understanding the issues. Following the Reformation period, several distinct schools of thought developed. Among conservative scholars, there were three major positions. First, there was Johannes Cocceius (1603-1669) who applied it to any Old Testament event or person that resembled a New Testament parallel. This came close to an allegorical approach. Secondly, there was John March (1757-1839) who asserted that the only types were those explicitly stated to be types in the New Testament. Thirdly, Patrick Fairbairn (1805-1874) mediated between the two by accepting both explicit and inferred types. With the rise of the historical-critical method in the nineteenth century, liberal scholarship rejected the unity between the Testaments and regarded typology as an inferior methodological approach to interpretation. Most modern liberal scholars continue to disregard typology altogether.

Neo-Orthodoxy

The neo-orthodox perspective understands typology as just more or less analogical thinking. An analogy is a comparison between two things that are similar in some way and is often used to help explain something or make it easier to understand. Within evangelicalism, the traditional view is that types occurred because God intentionally constructed pictures of Christ and then placed those pictures within Israel's history.

Issues In the Use of Typology

Typology represents a vital part of early Christian hermeneutics. It is built upon the belief that God unified his Word and the events of redemptive history. It is questioned whether typology is prospective (this refers to the Old Testament type as a divinely ordained prediction) or retrospective (this refers to the New Testament antitype as analogously related but not prefigured in the type). It is likely that the solution lies in the middle. The Old Testament authors and participants did not necessarily recognize any typological intent in the original. But in the divine plan, the early event did anticipate the later reality. Thus David's coronation (Ps. 2, 72, 110) did indeed foreshadow Jesus' enthronement as the royal Messiah, though it was not a direct prediction.

In many instances, the New Testament writers used the Old Testament in a typological manner. Typology, according to Terry, is defined in the following manner, "In the science of theology it properly signifies the preordained representative relation which certain persons, events and institutions of the Old Testament bear to corresponding persons, events, and institutions in the New."[65] Thus, types are pictures or object lessons by which God taught his people. Through types God teaches about his grace and the redemption he would provide through the Messiah. Such typology can be seen in the following passages:

- **Hosea 11:1 ~ Matthew 2:13-15 (note especially v. 15)**

"When Israel was a child, I loved him, and out of Egypt I called my son"—Hosea 11:1.

Now when they had departed, behold, an angel of the Lord appeared to Joseph in a dream and said, "Rise, take the child and his mother, and flee to Egypt, and remain there until I tell you, for Herod is about to search for the child, to destroy him." And he rose and took the child and his mother by night and departed to Egypt and remained there until the death of Herod. This was to fulfill what the Lord had spoken by the prophet, "Out of Egypt I called my son."—Matthew 2:13-15.

- **Isaiah 7:14 ~ Matthew 1:23**

"Therefore the Lord himself will give you a sign. Behold, the virgin shall conceive and bear a son, and shall call his name Immanuel."—Isaiah 7:14.

"Behold, the virgin shall conceive and bear a son, and they shall call his name Immanuel."—Matthew 1:23.

- **The priestly order: Jesus compared to Melchizedek in Hebrews 7:1-28**

For this Melchizedek, king of Salem, priest of the Most High God, met Abraham returning from the slaughter of the kings and blessed him, and to him Abraham apportioned a tenth part of everything. He is first, by translation of his name, king of righteousness, and then he is also king of Salem, that is, king of peace. He is without father or mother or genealogy, having neither beginning of days nor end of life, but resembling the Son of God he continues a priest forever. See how great this man was to whom Abraham the patriarch gave a tenth of the spoils! And those descendants of Levi who receive the priestly office have a commandment in the law to take tithes from the people, that is, from their brothers, though these also are descended from Abraham. But this man who does not have his

---

[65] Terry, *Biblical Hermeneutics*, 33.

descent from them received tithes from Abraham and blessed him who had the promises. It is beyond dispute that the inferior is blessed by the superior. In the one case tithes are received by mortal men, but in the other case, by one of whom it is testified that he lives. One might even say that Levi himself, who receives tithes, paid tithes through Abraham, for he was still in the loins of his ancestor when Melchizedek met him. Now if perfection had been attainable through the Levitical priesthood (for under it the people received the law), what further need would there have been for another priest to arise after the order of Melchizedek, rather than one named after the order of Aaron? For when there is a change in the priesthood, there is necessarily a change in the law as well. For the one of whom these things are spoken belonged to another tribe, from which no one has ever served at the altar. For it is evident that our Lord was descended from Judah, and in connection with that tribe Moses said nothing about priests. This becomes even more evident when another priest arises in the likeness of Melchizedek, who has become a priest, not on the basis of a legal requirement concerning bodily descent, but by the power of an indestructible life. For it is witnessed of him, "You are a priest forever, after the order of Melchizedek." For on the one hand, a former commandment is set aside because of its weakness and uselessness (for the law made nothing perfect); but on the other hand, a better hope is introduced, through which we draw near to God. And it was not without an oath. For those who formerly became priests were made such without an oath, but this one was made a priest with an oath by the one who said to him: "The Lord has sworn and will not change his mind, 'You are a priest forever.'" This makes Jesus the guarantor of a better covenant. The former priests were many in number, because they were prevented by death from continuing in office, but he holds his priesthood permanently, because he continues forever. Consequently, he is able to save to the uttermost those who draw near to God through him, since he always lives to make intercession for them. For it was indeed fitting that we should have such a high priest, holy, innocent, unstained, separated from sinners, and exalted above the heavens. He has no need, like those high priests, to offer sacrifices daily, first for his own sins and then for those of the people, since he did this once for all when he offered up himself. For the law appoints men in their weakness as high priests, but the word of the oath, which came later than the law, appoints a Son who has been made perfect forever.

- **King David (Psalm 22** selected **verses)**

[1] My God, my God, why have you forsaken me?

[6] ...scorned by mankind and despised by the people.

[7] All who see me mock me; they make mouths at me; they wag their heads;

[8] "He trusts in the LORD; let him deliver him; let him rescue him, for he delights in him!"

[14] I am poured out like water, and all my bones are out of joint; my heart is like wax; it is melted within my breast;

[15] my strength is dried up like a potsherd, and my tongue sticks to my jaws; you lay me in the dust of death.

[16] For dogs encompass me; a company of evildoers encircles me; they have pierced my hands and feet---

[17] I can count all my bones--- they stare and gloat over me;

[18] they divide my garments among them, and for my clothing they cast lots.

- **The entire sacrificial system which typified the ultimate sacrifice of God's Lamb (Jn. 1:29)**

Analogical

In several places, the New Testament writers interpreted Old Testament persons and events in an analogical sense. That is, the New Testament circumstances being like an Old Testament one. In this way, important events within the history of Israel are outlined or summarized in the life of Jesus (for example, Rachel weeping for her children in Mt. 2:16-18). It might be easy to accuse Matthew or any other New Testament writer of twisting Old Testament passages but, as D.A. Carson has said:

> Matthew is not simply ripping texts out of Old Testament contexts because he needs to find a prophecy in order to generate a fulfillment. Discernible principles govern his choices, the most important being that he finds in the Old Testament not only isolated predictions regarding the Messiah but also Old Testament history and people as paradigms that, to those with eyes to see, point forward to the Messiah.[66]

---

[66] D. A. Carson, *The Expositor's Bible Commentary: Matthew* (Vol.8), 77.

Thematic Parallels

The Gospel writers frequently developed messianic motifs that were present in the Old Testament. Jesus did this too (for example, such concepts as "Son of David" and "Son of Man" and the "Servant" idea in the book of Isaiah). Such thematic parallels would have been clearly understood by the early Jews. Their minds were steeped in the Hebrew Scriptures. They would have understood and appreciated the Messianic implications of redemptive history.

In some instances, an inaccuracy may seem apparent. This is because the New Testament author is citing the Septuagint (the Greek translation of the Old Testament) rather than the Hebrew text. This is not much different from contemporary Christians who might quote from a modern English translation in order to express a Scriptural point. It is natural that the Septuagint would be quoted as frequently as it is in the New Testament.[67] It was the most widely used translation in the Greek-speaking world of the first century. The New Testament writers employed a translation that was familiar to their readers. It would have been confusing if they had used the Hebrew manuscripts. Very few would have been able to read them.

Were the New Testament writers mistaken? Did Matthew misapply verses from the Old Testament by interpreting them as literal predictions of Jesus? What was the purpose in citing an Old Testament text? There are many reasons why they cited the Old Testament. The New Testament author may wish to confirm that a New Testament activity is in agreement with an Old Testament principle. He may wish to explain or clarify a point given in the Old Testament. He may wish to illustrate a New Testament truth or to provide the general sense of what the Old Testament said concerning the Messiah. He may wish to summarize an Old Testament concept or draw parallels between Israel and the Church. He may wish to provide warnings to New Covenant believers, show the progress of redemptive history, or demonstrate that Jesus is indeed the Messiah predicted in the Old Testament.

Resolving Alleged Discrepancies

Unbelieving critics claim that the Bible has numerous internal contradictions and factual errors. Any serious student of Scripture must face this. We must not avoid such thorny questions. We can face them

---

[67] In fact, the Septuagint, in some cases, has proven to more accurately reflect the thought of the original autographs than even the Masoretic text.

with confidence that the Bible is God's inerrant Word. God is a God of truth. He will not allow contradictions to corrupt its accuracy or undermine its authority. Here are some basic guidelines to aid the interpreter in resolving or harmonizing Bible difficulties.

1. Seeking plausible harmonization

Seeking a plausible solution or harmonization to difficult texts is not scholastic dishonesty. Harmonization is something which every literary critic engages in when studying texts of antiquity. This is true whether it be the writings of Homer, Josephus, or the Bible. According to Craig Blomberg, Associate Professor of New Testament at Denver Seminary, "All historians, whether they employ the term or not, practice some kind of harmonization as they seek to reconstruct the truth of past events ... [It is a] standard practice among secular historians of both written and oral traditions."[68] Thus, harmonization is not wrong. It is not an intellectually dishonest practice. Stein says:

> The terms harmonize and harmonization have fallen into disrepute. Some of this may be due to the farfetched and unconvincing harmonizations made in the past by certain scholars. This writer still remembers attending a graduate seminar at a famous German university where a student's explanation was rejected on the grounds that "Das ist nur Harmonizierung!" ("That is simply a harmonization!"). To reject an explanation because it harmonizes difficult gospel passages is certainly as prejudicial as to accept an explanation on the grounds that it harmonizes these passages. The correctness or incorrectness of an explanation is not dependent on whether or not it harmonizes the disputed passages. It depends on whether that explanation correctly interprets the authors' meanings and logically illustrates that these meanings do not conflict with each other.[69]

2. Answers and reasonable solutions

In the vast majority of cases (if not all), direct answers or reasonable solutions exist to problem passages. Such answers or harmonization are primarily found in conservative Bible commentaries. There are also specialized works, which treat Bible difficulties. Such as:

---

[68] Craig Blomberg, "The Legitimacy and Limits of Harmonization," *Hermeneutics, Authority, and Canon*, eds. D.A. Carson & John D. Woodbridge, (Wipf & Stock Pub; Reprint edition, 2005), 139, 144.

[69] Robert H. Stein, *Difficult Passages in the Gospels*, (Baker, 1984), 13.

- Gleason L. Archer, *Encyclopedia of Bible Difficulties* (Grand Rapids: Zondervan, 1982).

- Norman L. Geisler; Thomas Howe, *The Big Book of Bible Difficulties: Clear and Concise Answers from Genesis to Revelation* (Grand Rapids: Baker Books, 2008)

- Robert H. Stein, *Difficult Passages in the New Testament: Interpreting Puzzling Texts in the Gospels and Epistles* (Grand Rapids: Baker Book House, 1990).

- Walter Kaiser, F.F. Bruce, Manfred Brauch, Peter Davids, *Hard Sayings of the Bible* (Downers Grove, IL: Inter-Varsity Press, 1996).

- John W. Haley, *Alleged Discrepancies of the Bible* (Grand Rapids: Zondervan, 1977).

- David E. O'Brien, *Today's Handbook for Solving Bible Difficulties* (Minneapolis: Bethany House Publishers, 1990).

3. **When working through an apparent discrepancy, remember to apply hermeneutical basics.**

That is:

- Carefully study the context, historical background, and framework of the verse in dispute.

- Carefully study its grammar.

- Carefully study its relation to other passages in the Bible, which treat the same subject or doctrine.

4. **A large proportion of the <u>alleged</u> discrepancies in the Bible are traceable not to actual errors in the original manuscripts but to transmissional errors in the numerous manuscripts that we possess.**

Apparent discrepancies include:

- The variety of names applied to the same person or place.

- Different methods of reckoning times and seasons.

- Different local and historical standpoints.

- The special scope and plan of each particular book.

Terry's comments are helpful:

Variations are not contradictions, and many essential variations arise from different methods of arranging a series of particular facts. The peculiarities of oriental thought and speech often involve seeming extravagance of statement and verbal inaccuracies, which are of a nature to provoke the criticism of the less impassioned writers of the West. And it is but just to add that not a few of the alleged contradictions of Scripture exist only in the imagination of skeptical writers, and are to be attributed to the perverse misunderstanding of captious critics.[70]

5. The Bible itself mentions that some of its contents are, by nature, hard or perplexing (1 Cor. 13:12; 2 Pet. 2:16).

It should not surprise us when we come across difficult portions of Scripture, which challenges our thinking. Instead of throwing up our hands in frustration, we must labor diligently and prayerfully for the correct solution. Gleason Archer says there "is very little that God will long withhold from the surrendered heart and mind of a true believer."[71]

6. One of the reasons why apparent discrepancies exist in Scripture is man's fallible interpretations."

While the Bible authors were moved along by Holy Spirit and their autographs were perfect, absolutely error free, this is not so of copyist, and nor is it so of those who read and interpret the Scriptures. If there is a discrepancy, it is based on an imperfect human's imperfect interpretation, and will only be cleared up once he or she arrives at the correct interpretation. If we dig deeper into a text, it is likely that we will arrive at a mature understanding of the Word.

7. Another of the reasons why apparent discrepancies exist in Scripture is a wrong conception of the Bible.

On this, Edward D. Andrews writes:

> Many think that when we say the Bible is the Word of God, is of divine origin and authority, we mean that God is the speaker in every utterance it contains; but this is not what is meant at all. Oftentimes, it simply records what others say, i.e., what good men say, what bad men say, what inspired men say, what uninspired men say, what angels and demons say, and even what the devil says. The record of what they said is from God and absolutely true, but what those other persons are recorded as saying may be true or may not be true. It is true that they said it, but what they said may not be true.[72]

---

[70] Terry, *Biblical Hermeneutics*, 514.

[71] Gleason Archer, *Encyclopedia of Bible Difficulties*, (Zondervan, 1982), 15.

[72] Edward D. Andrews, *OVERCOMING BIBLE DIFFICULTIES Answers to the So-Called Errors and Contradictions*, (Christian Publishing House, 2015), 61.

He offers one such example, saying:

The devil is recorded in Genesis 3:4 as saying, "You will not surely die." It is true that the devil said it, but what the devil said is not true, but an infamous lie that shipwrecked our race. That the devil said it is God's Word, but what the devil said is not God's Word but rather, it is the devil's word. It is God's Word that this was the devil's word." He goes on to say, "It is very common to hear men quote what Eliphaz, Bildad or Zophar said to Job as if it were necessarily God's own words because it is recorded in the Bible, in spite of the fact that God disavowed their teaching and said to them, "you have not spoken of me what is right" (Job 42:7). It is true that these men said the thing that God records them as saying, but often they gave the truth a twist and said what is not right. A very large share of our difficulties thus arises from not noticing who is speaking. The Bible always tells us, and we should always note it.[73]

---

[73] Ibid., 61-62.

CHAPTER 9 The History of Biblical Hermeneutics

Until the Enlightenment, biblical hermeneutics was usually seen as a form of special hermeneutics. It was thought that Scripture required a special form of interpretation. In the nineteenth century, it became increasingly common to read Scripture just like any other writing. Schleiermacher argued against a distinction between "general" and "special" hermeneutics. He proposed a general theory of hermeneutics applicable to all texts, including the Bible.

Jewish Interpretation

There is evidence of interpretation and editing within the Old Testament (see Deut. 34:10). Ezra and his Levitical assistants explained the meaning of the Scriptures (Neh. 8). Did these returning exiles speak Hebrew? It could have been preserved as the language of their religion, but they were seventy years in captivity and must have spoken the language of Babylon.

Early Christianity regarded Jesus as the interpretive key to the Old Testament. They understood the Old Testament in messianic terms. The apostolic fathers engaged in both the instruction of converts and apologetics against Jewish critics. Church councils settled a disagreement between groups that could not otherwise come to an agreement. During the time of the Reformation, there was renewed interest and ability in Greek and Hebrew. There was a decline of interest and a growing criticism of the Vulgate and the doctrines derived from it. There was an increased reading of the Bible in the vernacular, English and German especially. Martin Luther asserted only Scripture has authority for the believer (*Sola Scriptura*). The Catholic response was to reaffirm tradition. Thus they reaffirmed the authority of the Vulgate.

Pietism

Pietism arose as a reaction to the focus on intellectual Protestant scholarship. Pietism was a movement within Lutheranism that lasted from the late seventeenth century to the mid-eighteenth century, and later. It influenced Protestantism and Anabaptism generally. It inspired Anglican priest John Wesley to begin the Methodist movement and Alexander Mack to begin the Brethren movement. The Pietist movement combined the Lutheranism of the time with the Reformed emphasis on individual piety. Pietism shares an emphasis on personal behavior with the Puritan movement, and the two are sometimes confused. But there are important differences, particularly in the concept of the role of religion in government.

Pietism was a reaction to dogmatism, scholasticism and formalism. Thus, it emphasized the need for a personal commitment to Christ. Within Pietism devotional, practical Bible study was stressed.

The Enlightenment

During the Enlightenment human reason sat in judgment over the authority of the church and ultimately over against the Bible. The dogmatism of Rationalism prevailed. It asserted that the human mind is an independent authority capable of determining truth. Spinoza (a Jewish/Dutch philosopher of the seventeenth-century and a forerunner of Enlightenment thinking) argued that the Bible should be studied as any other book. In this school of thought reason was supreme in studying the Bible.

Liberalism

The nineteenth century saw the rise of liberalism. There was increased confidence in scientific methods. The historical-critical method assumed that the use of human reason was the best tool to understand the Bible. This school of thought promoted the idea of reason free of theological constraints as a sufficient tool. The Bible was studied as any other text.

Friedrich Schleiermacher (1768–1834) was a German theologian, philosopher, and biblical scholar. He is known for his attempt to reconcile the criticisms of the Enlightenment with traditional Protestant Christianity. He also became influential in the evolution of Higher Criticism.

Higher Criticism (also known as Historical Criticism) is a branch of literary criticism that investigates the origins of ancient texts in order to understand "the world behind the text." The primary goal of historical criticism is to ascertain the text's original meaning in its original historical context. It aims to find and explicate the text's literal sense. It seeks to understand the historical situation of the author and recipients of the text. Thus an ancient text may serve as a record or source for reconstructing the ancient past. Schleiermacher's work forms part of the foundation of the modern field of hermeneutics. Because of his profound impact on subsequent Christian thought, he is often called the "Father of Modern Liberal Theology."

The Neo-Orthodox movement of the twentieth century (spearheaded by Karl Barth) was in many ways an attempt to challenge his influence. Higher criticism sought to understand the Bible purely as a human, historical document. The concept of hermeneutics acquired at least two different meanings ~ these are related but nevertheless distinct.

First, in the older sense, biblical hermeneutics may be understood as the theological principles of exegesis. In fact, it is often virtually synonymous with "principles of biblical interpretation" or "methodology of biblical exegesis." Second, the more recent development is to understand the term "biblical hermeneutics" as the broader underpinnings of interpretation. This relates to philosophy, linguistics, etc. Thus the question is posed: "How is understanding possible?" The rationale of this approach is that, while Scripture is more than just an ordinary text it is in the first instance a text. It is a text which human beings try to understand. In this sense, the principles of understanding any text apply to the Bible as well. They apply regardless of whatever other specifically theological principles one might want to consider in addition to that. In this second sense, then, all aspects of hermeneutics (philosophical, linguistic, etc.) are considered to be applicable to the biblical texts as well.

There are obvious examples of this in the links between twentieth-century philosophy and Christian theology. For example, Rudolf Bultmann's hermeneutical approach was strongly influenced by existentialism, in particular by the philosophy of Martin Heidegger. Since the 1960s the philosophical hermeneutics of Hans-Georg Gadamer has had a wide-ranging influence on biblical hermeneutics.[74]

Theological Hermeneutics as Traditional Christian Biblical Exegesis

This particular form of theological hermeneutics deals with various principles that can be applied to the study of Scripture. The canon of Scripture is an organic whole, rather than an accumulation of disparate individual texts.[75] So any interpretation that contradicts any other part of Scripture is not considered to be sound. Thus biblical hermeneutics differs from hermeneutics as generally understood. Within such traditional Protestant theology, there are a variety of interpretive formulae. These are generally not mutually exclusive. Therefore, interpreters may adhere to several of these approaches at once.

---

[74] Hans-Georg Gadamer was a German philosopher best known for his 1960 magnum opus, *Truth and Method*, on hermeneutics.

[75] See the chapter on canonicity.

The Historical-Grammatical Principle

This is based on historical, socio-political, geographical, cultural and linguistic contexts. This method is a Christian hermeneutics process which strives to discover the biblical author's original intended meaning in the text.[76] The process for determining the original meaning of the text involves an examination of the grammatical and syntactical aspects, the historical background, the literary genre and theological considerations. The historical-grammatical method identifies the one original meaning of the text and its significance. The significance of the text is essentially the application of the principles from the text.

The Original Meaning of Texts

The aim of the historical-grammatical method is to discover the meaning of the passage as the original author would have intended it. It is to discover the meaning as the original hearers would have understood. The original passage is seen as having only a single meaning or sense. Milton S. Terry has said:

> A fundamental principle in grammatico-historical exposition is that the words and sentences can have but one significance in one and the same connection. The moment we neglect this principle we drift out upon a sea of uncertainty and conjecture.[77]

Many practice the historical-grammatical method using the inductive method. This is a general three-fold approach to the text: 1) observation; 2) interpretation; 3) application.[78] Each step builds upon the other, and so they follow in order. The first step of observation involves an examination of words, structure, and literary forms. After observations are formed, then there is the second step. This is interpretation which involves asking questions and formulating answers to those questions. After the meaning is derived through interpretation, then there is the third step. This is application. Application involves determining both the theoretical and practical significance of the text and appropriately applying this significance to today's context. Technically speaking, the grammatical-historical method of interpretation is distinct from the

---

[76] Elwell, Walter A., *Evangelical Dictionary of Theology*, (Grand Rapids, Michigan: Baker Book House, 1984).

[77] Terry, Milton S., *Biblical Hermeneutics: a Treatise on the Interpretation of the Old and New Testaments*, (Grand Rapids Michigan: Zondervan, 1974), 205.

[78] Hendricks, Howard G., *Living by the Book* (Chicago: Moody Press, 1991), 349.

determination of the passage's significance in light of that interpretation. In other words, meaning and application are separate. Taken together, interpretation of the passage along with determining the meaning defines the term (biblical) hermeneutics.[79] We now need to compare this method briefly with other approaches to biblical interpretation.

Proof-Text Method

Prooftexting is the practice of using isolated quotations from the Bible to establish a proposition. All Bible scholars use isolated texts to share a biblical view. Even the apostle Paul in Romans Chapter 9 quotes eleven times from other parts of the Old Testament.[80] Forty plus authors wrote sixty-six book over a 1,600-year period, all of which make up one book. Therefore, if we are to understand what the Supreme author meant on a given subject, we must extract every verse that covers that subject, as long as it is contextually talking about the same thing, and we are not taking it out of context. None of the Bible authors was exhaustive on any subject. Where interpreters go wrong in their "bad proof-texting" is they take scriptures out of their context and twist them to fit their own personal ideas. Again, in the proof-text approach, verses and short sections of text are used to support a particular topic or position. Interpretations based on the proof-text method are often isolated from the context surrounding the verse. Critics claim it often neglects the historical setting and type of literary genre. The proof-text approach can be utilized in support of unorthodox teachings. In this method, applications tend to be allegorical in nature.[81]

Reader-Response Method

This is a postmodern form of literary criticism. It explores the capacity of the biblical texts to shape, revise or confirm the expectations readers bring to their reading of the text. This approach challenges the assumption of much of modern hermeneutics, which understands the main task of exegesis is to approach the text as a disinterested exegete. Reader-response theorists maintain that the reader and the text are

---

[79] Elwell, Walter A., *Evangelical Dictionary of Theology*, (Grand Rapids, Michigan: Baker, 1984), 565.

[80] The quotations are found in Romans chapter 9, verses 7 (Genesis 21:12), 9 (Genesis 18:14), 12 (Genesis 25:23), 13 (Malachi 1:2, 3), 15 (Exodus 33:19), 17 (Exodus 9:16), 25 (Hosea 2:23), 26 (Hosea 1:10), 27, 28 (Isaiah 10:22, 23), 29 (Isaiah 1:9), and 33 (Isaiah 28:16).

[81] Kaiser, Walter C., *An Introduction to Biblical Hermeneutics: The Search for Meaning* (Grand Rapids, Michigan: Zondervan, 1994), 31-32, 298.

interdependent. What is important then is not so much the intent of the original author of the text but the "conversation" between reader and text that emerges in the reading of the text.[82] In the reader-response method, the focus is on how the book is perceived by the reader ~ not on the intention of the author. So reader-response criticism is a school of literary theory that focuses on the reader (or audience) and his or her experience of a literary work. In contrast to other schools and theories that focus attention primarily on the author or the content and form of the work.

Literary theory has long paid some attention to the reader's role in creating the meaning and experience of a literary work. Modern reader-response criticism began in the 1960s and 1970s, particularly in America and Germany, in work by Norman Holland, Stanley Fish, Wolfgang Iser, Hans-Robert Jauss, Roland Barthes, and others. Important predecessors were I. A. Richards, who in 1929 analyzed a group of Cambridge undergraduates' misreadings. Louise Rosenblatt, who, in *Literature as Exploration* (1938), argued that it is important for the teacher to avoid imposing any preconceived notions about the proper way to react to any work and C. S. Lewis in *An Experiment in Criticism* (1961).

Reader-response theory recognizes the reader as an active agent who imparts "real existence" to the work and completes its meaning through interpretation. Reader-response criticism argues that literature should be viewed as a performing art in which each reader creates his or her own, possibly unique, text-related performance. It stands in total opposition to the theories of formalism and the New Criticism, in which the reader's role in re-creating literary works is ignored. New Criticism had emphasized that only that which is within a text is part of the meaning of a text. No appeal to the authority or intention of the author was allowed in the discussions of orthodox New Critics. No appeal to the psychology of the reader was allowed in the discussions of orthodox New Critics.

Kinds of Reader-Response Criticism

One can sort reader-response theorists into three groups. First, there are *individualists* who focus upon the individual reader's experience. Second, there are *experimenters* who conduct psychological experiments on a defined set of readers. Third, there are uniformists who assume a fairly uniform response by all readers. One can, therefore, draw a distinction between reader-response theorists who see the individual reader driving the whole experience and others who think of literary

---

[82] Stanley J. Grenz, David Guretzki & Cherith Fee Nordling, *Pocket Dictionary of Theological Terms* (Downers Grove, IL: InterVarsity Press, 1999), 99.

experience as largely text-driven and uniform (with individual variations that can be ignored). The most fundamental difference among reader-response critics is probably between those who regard individual differences among readers' responses as important and those who try to get around them.

In 1961, C. S. Lewis published *An Experiment in Criticism* where he analyzed the readers' role in selecting literature. He analyzed their selections in light of their goals in reading. Stanley Fish explored the reading tactics endorsed by different critical schools, introducing the idea of "interpretive communities" that share particular modes of reading. Richard Gerrig in the U.S. has experimented with the reader's state of mind during and after a literary experience. He has shown how readers put aside ordinary knowledge and values while they read ~ treating, for example, criminals as heroes. He has also investigated how readers accept, while reading, improbable or fantastic things (Coleridge's "willing suspension of disbelief") but discard them after they have finished.

In Canada, David Miall, usually working with Donald Kuiken, has produced a large body of work exploring emotional or "affective" responses to literature. They have used both experiments and new developments in neuropsychology. They have developed a questionnaire for measuring different aspects of a reader's response. There are many other experimental psychologists around the world exploring readers' responses, conducting many detailed experiments.[83] Two notable researchers are Dolf Zillmann and Peter Vorderer. Both work in the field of communications and media psychology. Both have theorized and tested ideas about what produces emotions such as suspense, curiosity, surprise etc. in readers.

Wolfgang Iser is a uniformist who asserts this response is controlled by the text. In his model, the text controls so that the reader's activities are confined within limits set by the literary work. Another important German reader-response critic was Hans-Robert Jauss, who defined literature as a dialectic process of production and reception. For Jauss, readers have a certain mental set, a "horizon" of expectations from which perspective each reader, at any given time in history, reads.

Objections

Reader-response critics hold that in order to understand a text, one must look to the processes readers use to create meaning and experience. Traditional text-oriented schools, such as formalism often think of reader-

---

[83] One can consult their work through their professional organizations, the International Society for the Empirical Study of Literature and Media, and International Association of Empirical Aesthetics, and through such psychological indices as PSYCINFO.

response criticism as anarchic, chaotic or lawless ~ showing no respect for established laws or rules. Traditional text-oriented schools, such as formalism often think of reader-response criticism as subjective ~ that is, allowing readers to interpret a text any way they want. Text-oriented critics claim that one can understand a text objectively and that one can understand a text while remaining immune to one's own culture, status and personality. To reader-response based theorists, however, reading is always both subjective and objective. Some reader-response critics (uniformists) assume a bi-active model of reading where the literary work controls part of the response, and the reader controls part. Individualists claim that the reader controls the whole transaction.

Another objection to reader-response criticism is that it fails to account for the text being able to expand the reader's understanding. Readers can and do put their own ideas and experiences into a work. They are at the same time gaining new understanding through the text. This is something that is generally overlooked in reader-response criticism. Some artworks are now purposely being fabricated which lack meaning. Such artworks are fabricated only to generate a "reader" response. If the reader response is guided and governed by interpretative communities, then the reader response rather than handing a freedom to the reader empowers the leaders of an interpretative community against the reader.

Research has shown that listening to emotionally intense parts of a story; readers respond with changes in heart rate. This indicates activity in the sympathetic nervous system.

Intense parts of a story were also accompanied by increased brain activity in a network of regions known to be involved in the processing of fear. Reader-response critics readily share the concerns of feminist critics and critics writing on behalf of gays, ethnic minorities, or post-colonial peoples. Everything can be processed through these interpretive grids.

Historical-Critical Method[84]

The historical-critical method is an interpretative technique employed by many academic biblical scholars in secular universities. It is also used by some Christian theologians. The method utilizes higher criticism in an attempt to discover the sources and factors that contributed to the making of the text. It seeks to determine what it meant to the original audience. The historical-critical method treats the Bible in the same way as other "human" texts. It embraces a naturalistic methodology and as such, for example, precludes interpretations, which allow prophetic foresight on

---

[84] Not to be confused with the historical grammatical method.

the part of the authors.[85] Historical-critical scholars are less interested in determining what the text means for people today. For these reasons, conservative Christians tend to reject the method.[86]

Trajectory Hermeneutics

This is also known as *Redemptive-Movement* hermeneutics. It is an approach within postmodern Christianity which suggests that parts of the Bible can have progressive, different meanings as a culture unfold, advances, and matures. One teaching under this view is that homosexuality was once a sin but has now become acceptable. This is due to cultural changes and advances in understanding of psychology and the social sciences. Advocates of trajectory hermeneutics may point to Romans 1:18-32 to say that Paul is speaking to those who violate their sexual orientation ~ that is those who go against their natural desire. But a homosexual's natural desire is for the same sex, which is now defended as natural by some.

One proponent of trajectory hermeneutics is William J. Webb, who says that the moral commands of the Bible were a significant improvement over the surrounding cultures. He says they were relevant to the Christians who lived at that time. He suggests that some such directives are possibly not for contemporary Christians.[87]

Biblical Hermeneutics

The Bible today is essentially the same as when it was originally written. We have upheld the historical-grammatical approach to hermeneutics. The essential question we have been examining is "how is meaning determined?" We have explored the importance of identifying what the author intended. We have spoken about the difference between *exegesis* and *eisegesis*. We are to draw out what is there, not to manipulate the text by projecting our views / opinions into it.

There is a need to bridge the gap between then and there and here and now. Every reader is an interpreter. Nobody approaches any text free

---

[85] Coogan, Michael D., *The Old Testament, a Historical and Literary Introduction to the Hebrew Scriptures*, (Oxford University Press, 2005).

[86] Farnell, F. David, Edward D. Andrews, Thomas Howe, Thomas Marshall, Benjamin Cocar, and Dianna Newman. *Basics of Biblical Criticism: Helpful or Harmful?* [Second Edition] (Cambridge, OH: Christian Publishing House, 2016).
http://www.christianpublishers.org/apps/webstore/products/show/5346435

[87] Webb, William J. *Slaves, Women and Homosexuals: Exploring the Hermeneutics of Cultural Analysis*, (Authentic Media, 2002).

of presuppositions or bias. There are certain assumptions (presuppositions) about the Bible's inspiration. According to the liberal view the Bible is a record of human concepts about God. The writers were inspired in the same way as Shakespeare. The conservative view asserts that God used the personalities of the writers in such a way as to provide the message that he wanted. The message is inspired (God-breathed). There is a difference of opinion among those who hold this view as to whether the Bible is inerrant in all its details (without error) or inerrant in all that it claims to teach regarding salvation and God's dealings with humanity. The latter position would allow for some historical, geographical, scientific, or numerical errors.

What are the implications of each position? If the latter position is taken, how can the Bible be trusted when it comes to matters regarding salvation, Christian living and morality? Most of the groups that have taken the latter position end up questioning teachings regarding salvation as well.

CHAPTER 10 Principles and Techniques of Biblical Interpretation

Principles

There are many principles that assist the interpreter in understanding the biblical text. For example, the covenant principle differentiates between the various contracts that God has made with his people, specifically their provisions, their parties and their purposes. The Christocentric principle helps us to understand that the mind of deity is eternally centered in Christ. All angelic thought and ministry are centered in Christ. All Satanic hatred is centered on Christ. All human hopes should be centered in Christ. The whole material universe is centered in Christ. The entire written Word is centered in Christ.

The context principle sheds light on a subject through either near or remote passages bearing upon the same subject.

The first mention principle strikes a keynote whereby the first mention of a subject indicates the mind of God on the matter.

The progressive mention principle is the idea that God makes the revelation of any given truth increasingly clear as the Word proceeds to its consummation.

In the full mention principle, God declares his full mind upon any subject vital to spiritual life.

The agreement principle is rooted in the truthfulness and faithfulness of God, which become the guarantee that his Word will not and cannot contradict itself.

In the direct statement principle, we understand that God says what he means and means what he says.

The threefold principle relates to how Scripture sets forth the truths of salvation in a three-fold way. First, there is the past ~ justification. Second, there is the present ~ sanctification / transformation. Third, there is the future ~ glorification / consummation.

The repetition principle should be noted because God repeats some truth or subject already given, perhaps with the addition of details not before given. There is a purpose to repetition ~ it is not a forgetful retelling of something or poor writing or editing of the biblical text.

The typical principle is about certain people, events, objects and rituals found in the Old Testament and how they may serve as object lessons and pictures. By these, God teaches us about his character, faithfulness, grace and saving power.

This not a comprehensive list of principles that aid interpretation but a sample of approaches, which act as interpretive keys.

Techniques

In the interpretation of a text, hermeneutics considers what language says, but it also considers what it supposes, doesn't say, and implies. The process consists of several steps for best attaining the Scriptural author's intended meaning.[88] With regard to the historical-grammatical approach to hermeneutics, we have said much about the historical and cultural element of that method, but we have said less about the grammatical or linguistic element. Linguistic analysis is central to this approach and is of immense importance. It is necessary to put words and phrases under the microscope, as it were, in order to gain a better understanding. With this in mind let us take an example of a word and process it through the lexical-syntactical grid to see what it yields.

Lexical-Syntactical Analysis

In a lexical-syntactical analysis, the order of the sentence such as punctuation and tense are important. Here, lexicons and grammar aids can help in extracting meaning from the text. This approach looks at the words used and the way the words are used.

Consider these words, "So, because you are lukewarm, and neither hot nor cold, I will spit you out of my mouth." (Rev. 3:16) We can clearly see that lukewarm attitudes are distasteful to Jesus. But if the text is examined more closely we discover that the message is more potent. It would be more accurate to say that lukewarm attitudes make the Lord sick, so much so that it induces nausea. Jesus does not say that he will *spit* them out of his mouth. This would imply that lukewarm attitudes are distasteful to him. Rather he says that he will vomit them out of his mouth. The idea is that lukewarm attitudes are utterly repulsive to Jesus. The implication (which is relevant to the application) is that if we lack zeal for the Lord we are backslidden.

The Greek word used here ἐμέω appears only once in the New Testament. It is transliterated as *emeó* which is a verb, and it means "to

---

[88] See Henry A Virkler, *Hermeneutics: Principles and Processes of Biblical Interpretation,* Baker Academic, 2007).

vomit." It does not mean, "to spit." The English word "emetic" is derived from it. An emetic is a drug often used to induce vomiting.

So properly, it means, "to vomit." This is an example of anthropomorphism which literally means "man form." It is figurative language by which God is described as having physical parts (e.g., eyes, hands, mouth, etc.), even though he is not a physical being (John 4:24; Luke 24:39). In fact, it is also an example of anthropopathism, which is a figure of speech by which human feelings or emotions are ascribed to God. This is in order to accommodate man's ignorance of the unfathomable intentions and operations of the deity (Romans 11:33-36).[89]

Therefore, the meaning of these words of Jesus to the church in Laodicea was figurative and very potent. Jesus was saying that he was repulsed by them and desired total separation from such lukewarm attitudes. He rejected such attitudes with extreme disgust. The message is clear: the Lord will not tolerate indifference and apathy. The Lord will not tolerate a mere outward show of respectability and religiosity.

The word ἐμέω (emeo ~ the verb to vomit) is not to be confused with the Greek word ἐξέραμα (exerama) which is the noun for vomit. This word also has only one occurrence in the New Testament where it appears in 2 Peter 2:22 "The dog returns to its own vomit." Neither is it to be confused with the Greek verb ἐμπτύω (emptuó), which means "to spit." This word (and it variants, spat, spitting...) appears six times in the New Testament. All refer to Jesus being spat on or predicting this. The word referring to Jesus spitting to heal (blind and deaf) is different.

Historical/Cultural Analysis

The history and culture surrounding the authors are important as it aids interpretation. This is especially true with regard to the relationship between Jews and Gentiles and more specifically with regard to the attitudes and teachings of Pharisees in relation to Gentiles.

See Appendix 3: The Pharisee and the Tax Collector

It is not only important to understand the Jewish sects of Palestine but also to have some knowledge of the government(s) that ruled Palestine in New Testament times. This increases understanding and enhances our appreciation of Scripture.

---

[89] Both Anthropomorphism and anthropopathism are mentioned in "Chapter 5: Keys to Understanding" and "Appendix 1: Does God Change His Mind?"

See Appendix 2: The Trial of Jesus

Special Literary Analysis

There are several special literary aspects to look at. But importantly each genre of Scripture has a different set of rules that applies to it. Of the genres found in Scripture, there are narratives, histories, prophecies, apocalyptic, poetry, epistles, wisdom, law, etc. In these, there are differing levels of figurative and literal language. Apocalyptic writings and poetry have more figurative language than narrative or historical writings. The genre must be recognized to gain a fuller understanding.

William D. Hendricks and Howard G. Hendricks in *Living by the Book* set out the method of observing, interpreting and applying the text.[90] Other major Christian teachers have based their hermeneutics on the principles Howard Hendricks teaches ~ people such as Chuck Swindoll (who wrote the foreword) and David Jeremiah.

David L. Barr states there are three obstacles that stand in the way of correctly interpreting the biblical writings. First, we speak a different language. Second, we live two millennia later. Third, we bring different expectations to the text ~ we approach the Bible with significantly different literary expectations than other forms of literature.[91]

---

[90] Howard G. G. Hendricks, William D. D. Hendricks, *Living By the Book: The Art and Science of Reading the Bible*, (Chicago: Moody Press, 1992).

[91] David L. Barr, *New Testament Story*, (Wadsworth Publishing, 1995), 15.

CHAPTER 11 Literary Forms

Poetry

Song of Songs

This book, also known as The Song of Solomon, it extols the beauty of romantic and sexual love. Some parts of the Bible are much better known than others. One of the more neglected parts of the Bible is the Song of Songs. It is rarely read and hardly ever used in preaching and as a consequence, it is not very well known. Such neglect is not good. This book was revealed for a purpose, and so it should not be neglected. It is beautifully poetic, but it also contains some very important lessons that God wants to communicate.[92]

The Song of Songs is poetical in form. Like all Hebrew poetry, it uses parallelism (see earlier section dealing with poetry). For example:

Song of Solomon 2:8

[8] Listen! My beloved!
   Behold, he is coming,
Climbing on the mountains,
   Leaping on the hills!

This kind of structure is quite unique in ancient literature. It survives translation into almost any language without much loss, unlike poetry based on rhyme or meter, which is challenging to translate and usually suffers a loss when translated from its native language. This is evident in some modern translations of the *Qur'an* where poetical structure, rhyme and meter have often been lost in translation from the original Arabic.

Primarily the Song of Songs is a song of praise celebrating the gift of love between a man and a woman. This is central to human life and experience. It is significant that God chose to deal with this topic through a poem. God did not present a long list of rules, regulations, and advice on this issue. Sexual love is a beautiful thing, which cannot be easily reduced to words on a page. Thus, the poetic form is suited to the content.

Down through the ages, both Jews and Christians alike have applied different interpretations to the book. For example, both Jews and Christians have suggested that the Song of Songs is an allegory. It has been said that it is a picture of God's love for his people Israel. It has been said that it is a picture of Christ's love for the Church. Elsewhere in the Bible,

---

[92] Song of Songs may also be classified as Wisdom literature.

the church is described as his "bride." Some have suggested that the Song of Solomon was originally written as a series of songs and that these were designed to be sung during a Jewish wedding feast.

It is important to understand that primarily the book is a dramatic poem. It has two or three characters (voices). First, there is the bride and her bridegroom (King Solomon). Second, there is the girl, her shepherd lover, and King Solomon (this is the more common understanding). Perhaps the most important question to ask when reading and trying to understand any part of the Bible is ~ what type of writing is this? What are the messages or themes that run through this poem?

The primary message of the book is that sexual love is a gift from God. In Western secular culture, sex is frequently cheapened and disengaged from love. It is often used as a marketing tool to sell products. The other extreme occurs in many Eastern cultures where women are hidden away behind closed doors.

The Song of Songs celebrates the joy of sexual love (within the context of a marriage relationship). The poem commends the shepherd and the maiden for their devoted love to one another. The maiden is praised for guarding her virtue and her virginity against all the advances of Solomon. She is saving herself for the one she loves and wants to marry. Yet sexual love is also commended in the poem as a gift from God to be celebrated. The Song of Songs celebrates true love:

> Set me as a seal upon your heart, as a seal upon your arm, for love is strong as death, jealousy is fierce as the grave. Its flashes are flashes of fire, the very flame of the LORD. Many waters cannot quench love, neither can floods drown it. If a man offered for love all the wealth of his house, he would be utterly despised.—Song of Songs 8:6-7.

We learn in the poem that by this time, Solomon had 140 wives and concubines. By the end of his reign, he had almost one thousand. But Scripture had specified laws concerning Israel's king, "And he shall not acquire many wives for himself, lest his heart turn away, nor shall he acquire for himself excessive silver and gold."—Deuteronomy 17:17.

Psalms

The psalms are a great comfort in times of discouragement. They were not written in a vacuum. They came out of the crucible of the real life experiences of the people of God. As such, they have an appealing authenticity. They are not the detached, theoretical reflections of religious philosophers. They are the prayers of real believers in the midst of real problems. They are the praises wrung out of real situations. They are quarried from real experience of God, often shaped and tempered in the furnace of affliction and hammered out on the anvil of life. They have much to offer by way of comfort in times of discouragement. They are a deep reservoir that will refresh the weary. There are many different types of psalms.

Classification of Psalms

- Lament Psalms ~ These express struggles, sufferings, disappointments.

- Imprecatory Psalms ~ These call down harm or curses (parts of 12, 35, 58, 59, 69, 70, 83, 109, 137, 140). On pastoral visits, I omit these sections! These express feelings directed to God, helping to channel anger. They help us to feel our anger, give it to God, and not act on it.

- Thanksgiving Psalms ~ These simply give thanks to God for the many blessings he bestows.

- Hymns of Praise ~ These praise God for what he has done and for who he is. These may contain a call to worship, with a response by the people (Ps. 118).

- Salvation-History Psalms ~ These review the history of Israel and how God has acted. For example, Psalm 136 contains brief references to events in Israelite history. Verses 5-9 are references to the biblical creation story. (Gen. 1:1-2:4a) Verse 11 begins a summary of the Exodus from Egypt and the conquest of Canaan. Verse 23 refers to the Babylonian Exile ~ "our low estate." Then verse 24 refers to the return from exile.

Psalms in the life of Israel

- Royal psalms (2, 18, 20, 21, 45, 72, 101, 110, 144).

- Enthronement Psalms (24, 29, 47, 93, 95-99).

- Liturgical Psalms ~ The liturgical Psalms were used in special festivals or services of worship in the life of ancient Israel. For example, the Royal Psalms (listed above) likely had their original setting in the coronation of Israel's king. They were preserved and adapted to other uses long after the monarchy came to an end. The remnants of their original purpose are often obvious. This helps us understand some of the features in the Psalms.

- Covenant Psalms (40, 81). These are covenant renewal liturgies which may have had their original setting in an annual covenant renewal ceremony.

- Songs of Zion (46, 48, 76, 84, 87, 122). The Songs of Zion and the temple liturgies could be used for any of several festivals celebrated in Jerusalem. On the occasion of the triumphal entry of Christ into Jerusalem the action of the crowd was completely spontaneous. They proclaim "Hosanna" as a customary greeting or blessing to welcome pilgrims during the Passover festivities. It is taken from Psalm 118:26 which is a liturgical psalm.

- Wisdom Psalms (36, 37, 49, 73, 112, 127, 128, 133)

- Songs of Trust ~ These focus on the fact that God can be trusted (11, 16, 23, 27, 2, 63, 91, 121, 125, 131).

As Christians, we use the psalms to inform and guide our worship. They are very helpful in terms of showing us how to relate honestly to God. They draw us in to meditate and reflect on God and his Word.

Wisdom Books

The wisdom books are Job (in narrative form), Ecclesiastes, Proverbs (in poetic form, pithy sayings, and examples of parallelism, etc.) and Song of Songs (in poetic form). What is the nature of wisdom literature? Essentially wisdom literature is concerned with godly living and as such it is practical. They are focused on how to make godly choices in life.

Wisdom literature directs us to know God: obey him and commit to him. These books are sometimes used inappropriately. There is a tendency to read only bits and pieces, rather than extended passages. People tend to do this because of the diversity of topics, even within a short section. But this leads to wrenching things out of context.

It is important to understand the proper use of terms such as "fool," which does not mean a stupid person. Rather it means one who does not believe in God and is therefore deemed to be morally deficient.

Wisdom literature often gives lines of thinking that are incorrect from God's point of view. Ecclesiastes and Job are good examples. Wisdom literature does not cover all aspects of life. Wisdom was taught both in society and in the home. Its goal was obedience to God's teaching. By describing how to live, it encouraged proper living. By making statements about the consequences of wrong living, it discouraged wrong living. Proverbs is about practical attitudes toward godly living. It contrasts choosing a life of wisdom and a life of folly.

Ecclesiastes

The book of Ecclesiastes is dripping with cynicism. This book views life from the vantage point of this earthly life. The author repeatedly asserts that life is meaningless, but he cannot live with this conclusion. Hints that show the true meaning of life are found in chapter eight.

> When I applied my heart to know wisdom, and to see the business that is done on earth, how neither day nor night do one's eyes see sleep, then I saw all the work of God, that man cannot find out the work that is done under the sun. However, much man may toil in seeking, he will not find it out. Even though a wise man claims to know, he cannot find it out.—Ecclesiastes 8:16-17.

Wisdom is not discovered, it is disclosed. It is not by means of man's speculation but by means of God's revelation that wisdom is obtained. People who live apart from God's Word cannot discover the meaning of life. The true meaning of life must go beyond what we can see and observe.

Solomon states that he diligently engaged in the search for wisdom (Eccles. 1:13). The Book of Ecclesiastes is the result of the author's studies conducted by human wisdom. In his investigations and explorations, Solomon encounters much that is "meaningless." It seems that every path the author takes is futile.

However, in the end, Solomon does reach a path that leads to meaningfulness. Thus he states, "The end of the matter; all has been heard. Fear God and keep his commandments, for this is the whole duty of man. For God will bring every deed into judgment, with every secret thing, whether good or evil." (Eccl. 12:13-14). One author has said of Ecclesiastes, "The scope of Ecclesiastes is to contrast the vanity of all mere human pursuits, when made the chief end, as contrasted with the real blessedness of true wisdom."[93] Charles Bridges says:

> "...to bring out into clear view the chief good ~ the true happiness of man, in what it does not consist ~ not in the wisdom, pleasures, honours, and riches of this world ~ in what it does consist ~ the enjoyment and service of God...Solomon's [sic] is not to allure men to the pleasures of the world, but rather to deter them from such pleasures, and exhort them with a Divine eloquence to despise the world. After having disputed through the whole book against those who desire to satisfy themselves with such good, he at the close teaches them that happiness consisteth not in things of this kind, but in true piety

---

[93] Jamieson, Fausset, and Brown's *Commentary On the Whole Bible*, Vol. IV, (Zondervan, 1999), xvi.

~ and thus concludes, Fear God, and keep His commandments; for this is the whole of man."[94]

To understand that the Book of Ecclesiastes is written from a human point of view is crucial to the understanding of the book. If this is not understood properly, there are many passages in the book which truly sound strange and out of place for inclusion in an inspired book of the Bible. For example, the author writes, "Be not overly righteous, and do not make yourself too wise." (Eccl. 7:16). In addition, "Bread is made for laughter, and wine gladdens life, and money answers everything."—Ecclesiastes 10:19.

For the most part, Solomon is not so much telling us how things should be, but how things are. He recounted what he has seen and experienced as he pursued earthly wisdom ("under the sun"). Invariably, as Solomon follows worldly pursuits ~ worldly wisdom, worldly pleasures and the like, he finds it all ultimately meaningless. Yet, there is a purpose to all this apparent negativity. As Derek Kidner points out, "He is demolishing to build."[95] In order to truly appreciate the wisdom of God, we must realize the futility of human wisdom, without God. Solomon's discourse strikes a chord. Kidner says, "The searching questions he has asked are those that life itself puts to us."[96]

Much of the perspective presented in Ecclesiastes is from a worldly point of view. It raises universal and transcendent questions about the meaning and purpose of life. It is a book that stimulates spiritual reflection and makes the reader ponder these things and wonder at the perceived meaninglessness of life. Since these issues resonate in the lives of believers and non-believers, this book can be valuable as a tool for exploring the meaning of life. Many are seeking an answer to the questions that Solomon raises.

The book of Ecclesiastes reveals that God knows and understands the things people ponder about life. God knows and understands the hearts of people. He knows what they feel and think. The end result of pursuing godless "wisdom" is to encounter meaninglessness and despair. The book of Ecclesiastes reveals that God understands the human condition.

Much of the perspective in Ecclesiastes is cynical, but ultimately it presents truth. At the end of Ecclesiastes, the author states, "The Preacher sought to find words of delight, and uprightly he wrote words of truth."

---

[94] Charles Bridges, A Commentary on Ecclesiastes, (Geneva Series, Banner of Truth, 1960), xii, xiii-xiv.

[95] Derek Kidner, The Message of Ecclesiastes, (IVP Academic, reprint edition, 1984), 19.

[96] Ibid.

(Eccl. 12:10) Ecclesiastes eloquently expresses the existential questions that we face here on earth. The book presents the reader with the *meaninglessness* of life from a secular and temporal point of view in order to attract the reader to the *meaningfulness* of life from a transcendent and truly spiritual perspective.

Job

The book of Job contains bad advice and incorrect conclusions about God and the way he works. It depends on who is speaking in the book. Job himself has a godly perspective, but his three comforters do not and neither does his wife. This book teaches that "bad" things happen to good and godly people. Life is not "fair." God's ways are beyond our ways. The book portrays the sovereignty of God, the problem of pain and the beauty of faith.

Job is one of the most difficult books to understand in the Bible and is almost entirely poetry, making interpretation even more challenging. Of the seven voices (Narrator, Job, Eliphaz, Bildad, Zophar, Elihu, and the LORD), all save the Narrator are presented as somewhat lengthy discourses or speeches. At first glance, Job's discourses appear to contradict the teaching of other parts of the Bible (e.g., see chapter 24, where Job describes the widespread injustice on the earth, asking why the Almighty doesn't appear to be doing anything about it) and the discourses of his friends appear to draw support from other parts of the Bible (e.g., see Bildad's response in chapter 25, upholding the righteousness and power of God), yet at the end of the book, the LORD says that Job has spoken correctly and his friends have not. Here are some points to bear in mind when reading the book of Job.

Job and his three "counsellors" had an oversimplified, and therefore incorrect view of the Lord's justice and mercy. Job's focus was on the Lord's mercy, whereas the focus of his "friends" was on the LORD's justice. Both views were partially incorrect. Job equated obedience as the requirement to receive the Lord's mercy, which in practical terms for Job was his wealth and abundance of blessings. Job's friends distorted the cause and effect. They saw that misfortune befell Job and reasoned that it must have resulted from Job's sin ~ which they had not witnessed.

Job's discourses are mainly remonstrations (expressing earnest opposition or protest), which people who are suffering may experience as they process what is happening to them. His friend's responses, though well intended, are actually inaccurate and unhelpful. Their perspective is more harmful than helpful to Job. Although Job remonstrated with God, he never repudiated his faith in the Lord. The misunderstandings of Job's friends are blasphemous because they make the LORD the author of suffering.

The greatest challenge in reading Job is discerning which passages are the "incorrect" views and which are the correct, for all five of the human voices (Job, Eliphaz, Bildad, Zophar and Elihu) contain errors about the LORD's mercy and justice.

Narrative

The Bible contains more narrative than any other kind of material. That does not mean that they are fiction. We use the word "narrative" to refer to a story with a set of characters and plot. The purpose of the Bible's narrative is to show God's work in history. It is important to know what narratives are and what they are not. They are not *just* stories about people. They are stories about God's actions *to* and *through* those people. So, a story in which Abraham features is not so much about Abraham as it is about the God of Abraham. It is not always easy to understand why God worked the way he did.

Narratives are limited in scope. We should not read more into the stories than the stories warrant. Narratives do not teach directly in a didactic sense, but they do illustrate truth. By combining narrative with explicit teaching, we get a better understanding of what God wants us to know.

There are different levels of narrative. Each level is part of the level above it, and should be examined as to how it helps to advance the upper level. At the top level, there is the story of the entire Bible ~ redemptive history. The middle level deals mostly with Israel, then Jesus and the church. At the bottom level, there are individual narratives.

There are accounts or reports of battles, and there are dreams, epiphanies, historical stories, and memoirs. In terms of understanding biblical narratives, an epiphany is a sudden leap of understanding, especially through an ordinary but striking occurrence. So, in the Biblical sense, an epiphany is sometimes caused by an angel (or a "manifestation of God") appearing and imparting some information. In the New Testament, the classic epiphany is Paul on the road to Damascus. In the Old Testament, it might be the burning bush that Moses encountered.

The Bible contains heroic narrative centered around the lives of characters such as Moses, Joseph, Daniel, and David ~ to mention just a few. The epic narratives are the historical narratives of a virtuous hero or of the origins of a group (Israel), or of the world (the Flood). The prophet stories describe the lives of the prophets and what may be emulated (Elijah, Daniel) or avoided (Jonah). Sometimes narratives trace how the tragedy turns to triumph. This is evidenced in the life of the Old Testament character, Joseph. In narrative character, development (or decline) is also important. We must interrogate the narrative to get at the core issues. What role does God play? Direct, indirect? What are the main themes, and what applications can be drawn? In terms of preaching, narratives are engaging inasmuch as people can relate to the trials and difficulties in the lives of the biblical characters. The apostle Paul, in issuing warnings about idolatry says, "Now these things happened to them as an example, but they were written down for our instruction…" This refers to narratives as well as the law.

Law

Law usually refers to the first five books of the Old Testament or to the commands that are found in Exodus through to Deuteronomy, particularly the Ten Commandments. What is the Christian relationship with the Law? That's the crucial question. The Old Testament Law is God's covenant ~ an agreement with Israel and it has three distinct dimensions: moral (absolute and universal), ceremonial (superseded by Christ) and judicial (temporal punishments relating to specific breaches of the law, which could be legitimately imposed by the ruling authorities in Israel at that time).

Obedience to the Law demonstrated loyalty to God. Parts of the Old Covenant are renewed or repeated in the New. The Old Testament is the Word of God. Many Christians tend to neglect it in their devotional lives, and many preachers avoid it. What can we learn from it? We learn the sorts of things that God wants from his people and indeed all people. We learn that God favors justice that is fair and not partial. God wants his people to be separate from sin and pagan practices and to have a dynamic relationship with him.

Gospel

We all know the word gospel means "good news." We all know the Gospels were not written by Jesus, they were written about him. Why four, especially since three of them are so similar? They were written for specific audiences with particular needs. The Gospels are not exactly biographies in the modern sense. They are similar to Hellenistic biographies. These focused on specific events, deeds, and sayings of a person's life, to teach certain lessons. The death of a person was a particular focus. They are theological biographies.

Are they trustworthy? The Gospels quote freely and give abbreviations of speeches. They arrange material topically or geographically rather than chronologically. The material is selected to fulfill the authors' purposes. We should always compare parallel passages and examine how each author deals with the material. This is more important when reading the synoptic gospels.[97] Material should be interpreted within the structure and themes of its own gospel. The Gospels should be read in paragraphs or periscopes (sections).

Necessary Background

Some study of the Second Temple (inter-testament) period is necessary to understand Palestine and the Judaism of the day as well as Greco-Roman backgrounds and geography. A key question is ~ to whom were the Gospels originally addressed? Mark was probably addressed to a Gentile audience that needed encouragement because of persecution. John downplays the role of John the Baptist, perhaps because some were exalting him. There are key theological issues in the Gospels ~ such as the Kingdom of God: its arrival, its nature, its citizens, how to enter it.[98]

Stories In the Gospels

Are we to understand the miracle stories literally? Or should we demythologize these stories and seek the theological truth behind the story by stripping away myths (as some would suggest) that surround the truths? Was the feeding of the five thousand (Mk. 6:30-44) just a moral lesson about a boy sharing his picnic? The miracle stories demonstrated who Jesus was. They verify that God was in fact acting in history. The miracles were performed so that Jesus and his claims would challenge people.

In the gospels, there are different kinds of stories. For example, there are pronouncement stories (Mk. 2:13-17 ~ the calling of Levi) which contain a story that ends with Jesus' statement about why he came, "Those who are well have no need of a physician, but those who are sick. I came not to call the righteous, but sinners." (Mk. 2:17).

Other forms may be categorized as follows:

- Beatitudes
- Woes
- Farewell Discourses
- Various Figures of Speech
- Narrative

---

[97] The gospels of Matthew, Mark, and Luke are referred to as the Synoptic Gospels because they include many of the same stories, often in a similar sequence and in similar wording. They stand in contrast to John, whose content is comparatively distinct.

[98] Gordon D. Fee and Douglas Stuart, *How to Read the Bible for All It's Worth: A Guide to Understanding the Bible*, (Grand Rapids: Zondervan, 1982), 131, 133.

Acts

We have already had an extensive discussion about what is and what is not normative in the book of Acts and for that reason I will keep my comments here brief. The book of Acts, like any other book of Scripture, needs to be handled with due care and attention. We should carefully examine what is consistent with teaching in other biblical passages. Is there a specific directive elsewhere? What is said consistently about certain things? What patterns are present? The fact that something did happen is no authority for believing that it should happen again. We must decide what is central to the narrative and what is *incidental* in detail. *Incidental* in detail does not mean *irrelevant* or *insignificant*.

The book of Acts is similar in many ways to Luke. It is history, but it is also a "Gospel" of sorts. We should treat Luke and Acts as a unit. Acts is best understood as theological history (similar to the books of Kings and Chronicles). We need to be sensitive to Luke's theological emphases. He traces the history of Christianity and outlines Paul's ministry from Jerusalem to Rome. This is one of the major themes of Acts. Luke is interested in how the Christian movement became predominantly Gentile. Luke appears to be historically accurate.

Epistles

The epistles may not be as straightforward as they seem in terms of application today. Consider 1 Corinthians 5 and the issues surrounding the excommunication of someone when they can easily go to another nearby church. The epistles are more than personal correspondence. They contain a significant amount of didactic (teaching) material. They may deal with a subject systematically and extensively, but they are not theology textbooks. There is "occasional" material which must be interpreted in light of the occasions that gave rise to them. So they contain first-century occasional material directed at specific issues. The theology present in the Epistles is not exhaustive. It is primarily directed to the task at hand (countering a heresy, correcting an error...). To properly understand them we must, as much as possible, understand what gave rise to the letter. We know the answer, but we must figure out what the question or problem was.[99]

Literary Forms In the Epistles

Most letters began with a salutation. Is there any significance in the order "Grace and peace" in these salutations? One could argue that the latter issues from the former. When a New Testament letter differs from

---

[99] Gordon D. Fee and Douglas Stuart, *How to Read the Bible for All It's Worth*, 48.

the norm, it is important to take note. There are various types of letters. Some are diatribes which attempt to answer hypothetical objections from opponents. There are letters to individuals and letters to churches. Then there are epistles that are not like letters, such as Hebrews, which does not have a salutation, but there is a benediction and final greetings. The first epistle of John does not have a greeting and neither does it have the kind of closure one might expect from an epistle. However, it does contain the statement: "I write these things to you who believe in the name of the Son of God that you may know that you have eternal life" (1 Jn. 5:13). These may have been homilies or meditations.

Within an epistle, there may be domestic codes that describe what people within families or the church should or should not do. These are addressed to those in authority as well as subordinates.—Ephesians 5:22-6:9.

There are sometimes slogans in the epistles, which are not always easy to recognize. There are a number of these in 1 Corinthians (e.g. 6:12) and in other epistles (e.g. Rom. 14:20).

There are vice and virtue lists that describe proper and improper behavior (see the vice list in 1 Timothy 1:8 ff. and Galatians 5:19 ff. and the virtue list in Galatians 5:22 ff.).

There are significant theological issues in the Pauline epistles. The center of Pauline theology is justification by faith. This challenged the Jews of his day with their nationalistic pride and exclusivity.

Interpreting Epistles

When it comes to interpreting the epistles, it is important to understand the historical context and, therefore, advisable, to use a Bible dictionary, encyclopedia, and commentaries. Read the entire Epistle at one sitting. Do this several times, taking brief notes as you go. Read it in different translations. Begin to make an outline of the letter, dividing it into big chunks first. The sub-headings are usually helpful. In terms of literary context think paragraphs rather than verses. As you read, summarize each paragraph in a sentence or two. What is being said, and why? The letter cannot mean what it did not mean for the original readers or author. When the situation is different, then we must try to derive a principle (which is consistent with the original principle) that may be applied.

CHAPTER 12 Canonicity

It is all very well to assert, as we do, that the Bible is the inspired, inerrant Word of God. Holding such a view, in turn, leads us to accept Scripture as authoritative in all matters of faith and practice. It is imperative, therefore, that we have an understanding of the canonicity of the Bible.[100]

What is the canon of scripture? Canonicity refers to the books that belong in Scripture. The canon refers to the writings that are regarded as authentic. It is, therefore, the body of Scripture, as we know it ~ 39 books of the Old Testament and 27 books of the New Testament. The word "canon" comes from Greek and Hebrew words that literally mean "measuring rod." A canonical book is one that measures up to the standard of Holy Scripture by meeting certain requirements. So the canon of Scripture refers to the books that are considered to be the authoritative Word of God.

How do we know that the 66 books of our Bible are the only inspired books? Who decided which books were truly inspired by God? The Roman Catholic Bible includes books that are not found in the Protestant Bible. These are called the *Apocrypha*. How do we know that Protestants have the right books? These questions are addressed by a study of canonicity. So, canonicity describes the standard that books had to meet to be recognized as Scripture.

On the one hand, deciding which books were inspired seems like a human process. Christians gathered together at church councils in the first several centuries A.D. for the purpose of officially recognizing which books were inspired. But it is important to remember that these councils did not determine which books were inspired. They simply recognized or ratified what God had already determined.

What tests of canonicity were used? What is the history of canonicity? Why are certain disputed books deemed not to be Scripture? The collection of 66 books was properly recognized by the early church as the complete, authoritative Scriptures not to be added to or subtracted from in any way.

---

[100] Although the issues of canonicity more correctly belong to the field of bibliology rather than hermeneutics, I think the journey from hermeneutics to homiletics should encompass the matter of canonicity and that is why this chapter is included.

Tests of canonicity

The early church councils must have applied certain standards in recognizing whether a book was inspired or not. We are not sure what these criteria were. However, they might have focused on things such as:

1. Is it authoritative ("Thus says the Lord")?

2. Is it prophetic ("a man of God" 2 Peter 1:20)?

A book in the Bible must have the authority of a spiritual leader of Israel. In the Old Testament, that is a prophet, king, judge or scribe. In the New Testament, it must be based on the testimony of an original apostle. In assessing the validity of each book there are important questions, such as:

3. Is it authentic (consistent with other revelation of truth)?

4. Is it dynamic ~ demonstrating God's life-changing power? (Heb. 4:12)?

5. Is it received (accepted and used by believers, historically? (1 Thess. 2:13)?

Old Testament

There are some guidelines for recognizing the correct books.

1. Christ refers to Old Testament books as "Scripture" (Mt. 21:42, etc.).

2. Josephus, the Jewish historian (A.D. 95), indicated that the 39 books were recognized as authoritative.

The Council of Jamnia

It has often been put forward that The Council of Jamnia (A.D. 90) officially recognized our 39 Old Testament books. But there is a problem with the credibility of this. The Council of Jamnia, presumably held in Jamnia (or *Yavne* in Hebrew), Israel was a hypothetical late first-century council at which the canon of the Hebrew Bible was alleged to have been finalized. First proposed by Heinrich Graetz in 1871, this theory was popular for much of the twentieth century. However, it was increasingly questioned from the 1960s onward, and the theory has been largely discredited.[101]

---

[101] See, for example, Jack P. Lewis "Jamnia Revisited" in Lee Martin McDonald (Editor), James A. Sanders (Editor), *The Canon Debate*, (Hendrickson; Reprint edition, 2002).

The Talmud relates that sometime before the destruction of the Second Temple in A.D. 70 Rabbi Yohanan ben Zakkai relocated to the city of Yavneh/Jamnia, where he received permission from the Romans to found a school of *halakha* (Jewish religious law).

The *Mishnah* (an authoritative collection of exegetical material embodying the oral tradition of Jewish law and forming the first part of the Talmud), compiled at the end of the second-century A.D. describes a debate over the status of some books of *Ketuvim*, and in particular over whether or not they render the hands "impure."[102] *Yadaim* 3:5 calls attention to a debate over Song of Songs and Ecclesiastes.[103] The *Megillat Taanit*[104], in a discussion of days when fasting is prohibited but that are not noted in the Bible, mentions the holiday of *Purim*.[105] Based on these, and a few similar references, Heinrich Graetz concluded in 1871 that there had been a Council of Jamnia which had decided the Jewish canon sometime in the late first- century (c. 70–90).[106]

W. M. Christie was the first to dispute this popular theory in the July 1925 edition of *The Journal of Theological Studies* in an article entitled "The Jamnia Period in Jewish History." Jack P. Lewis wrote a critique of the popular consensus in the April 1964 edition of the *Journal of Bible and Religion* entitled "What Do We Mean by Jabneh?" Sid Z. Leiman made an independent challenge for his University of Pennsylvania thesis published later as a book in 1976. Raymond E. Brown largely supported Lewis in his review published in the *Jerome Biblical Commentary* (also appears in the *New Jerome Biblical Commentary* of 1990), as did Lewis' discussion of the

---

[102] *Ketuvim* is the third and final section of the *Tanakh* (Hebrew Bible), after *Torah* (instruction) and *Nevi'im* (prophets). In English translations of the Hebrew Bible, this section is usually entitled "Writings" or "Hagiographa."

[103] *Yadayim* ("Hands") a treatise of the *Mishnah* and the *Tosefta* (a compilation of the Jewish oral law from the late second-century, the period of the Mishnah, dealing with the uncleanness of the hands and their ablution).

[104] *Megillat Taanit* (Hebrew: תענית מגילת) is chronicle which enumerates 35 eventful days on which the Jewish nation either performed glorious deeds or witnessed joyful events. These days were celebrated as feast-days. Public mourning was forbidden on 14 of them, and public fasting on all.

[105] *Purim* is a Jewish holiday that commemorates the saving of the Jewish people from Haman, who was planning to kill all the Jews. This took place in the ancient Persian Empire. See Book of Esther.

[106] Albert C. Sundberg, Jr. "The Old Testament of the Early Church Revisited." http://department.monm.edu/classics/Speel_Festschrift/sundbergJr.htm ~ Accessed 16 November, 2015. This document is part of the Festschrift in Honor of Charles Speel, edited by Thomas J. Sienkewicz and James E. Betts and published by Monmouth College in Monmouth, Illinois in 1997.

topic in 1992s *Anchor Bible Dictionary*.[107] Albert C. Sundberg Jr. summarized the crux of Lewis' argument as follows:

> Jewish sources contain echoes of debate about biblical books but canonicity was not the issue and debate was not connected with Jabneh...Moreover, specific canonical discussion at Jabneh is attested only for Chronicles and Song of Songs. Both circulated prior to Jabneh. There was vigorous debate between Beth Shammai and Beth Hillel over Chronicles and Song of Songs; Beth Hillel affirmed that both "defile the hands." One text does speak of official action at Jabneh. It gives a blanket statement that "all Holy Scripture defile the hands," and adds "on the day they made R. Eleazar b. Azariah head of the college, the Song of Songs and Koheleth (Ecclesiastes) both render the hands unclean"(M. Yadayim 3.5). Of the apocryphal books, only Ben Sira is mentioned by name in rabbinic sources and it continued to be circulated, copied and cited. No book is ever mentioned in the sources as being excluded from the canon at Jabneh.[108]

According to Lewis:

> The concept of the Council of Jamnia is an hypothesis to explain the canonization of the Writings (the third division of the Hebrew Bible) resulting in the closing of the Hebrew canon. ... These ongoing debates suggest the paucity of evidence on which the hypothesis of the Council of Jamnia rests and raise the question whether it has not served its usefulness and should be relegated to the limbo of unestablished hypotheses. It should not be allowed to be considered a consensus established by mere repetition of assertion.[109]

Other scholars have since joined in and today the theory is largely discredited.

New Testament

1. The apostles claimed authority for their writings (Col. 3:16; 1 Thess. 5:27; 2 Thess. 3:14).
2. The apostle's writings were equated with Old Testament Scripture (2 Pet. 3:1, 2, 15, 16).
3. The Council of Athanasius (A.D. 367) and the Council of Carthage (A.D. 397) recognized the 27 books in our New Testament today as inspired.

---

[107] *Anchor Bible Dictionary* Vol. III, (New York 1992), 634–7.

[108] Albert C. Sundberg, Jr. "The Old Testament of the Early Church Revisited."

[109] Jack P. Lewis "Jamnia Revisited," in McDonald & Sanders (editors), *The Canon Debate*, 2002.

Although the New Testament does not speak of a completed canon of Scripture, it does testify to writings already considered to be the Word of God. Peter recognized the writings of the Apostle Paul as Scripture. He cited Paul's letters, which some were twisting "as they do the rest of the Scriptures" (2 Pet. 3:15, 16). When Paul wrote to Timothy he quoted a passage from the Gospel of Luke as Scripture, "For the Scripture says, you shall not muzzle an ox while it treads the grain," and, "the laborer is worthy of his wages." (1 Tim. 5:18). The first verse quoted is from Deuteronomy, but the second is a quotation of one of our Lord's statements recorded by Luke, "The laborer is worthy of his wages."—Luke 10:7.

Disputed Non-Canonical Books

The Apocryphal books are not Scripture. The Apocryphal books are 15 books written in the 400 years between Malachi and Matthew. They record some of the histories of that time period and various other religious stories and teaching. The Catholic Bible includes these books as Scripture. The Apocrypha includes some specific Catholic doctrines, such as:

- purgatory and prayer for the dead (2 Maccabees 12:39-46)

- Salvation by works (almsgiving – Tobit 12:9).

Interestingly, the Catholic Church officially recognized these books as Scripture in A.D. 1546. That is only 29 years after Martin Luther criticized these doctrines as unbiblical. Here are several additional reasons why the Apocrypha have been rejected:

1. The Jews never accepted the Apocrypha as Scripture.

2. The Apocrypha never claims to be inspired ("Thus says the Lord" etc.)

3. The Apocrypha is never quoted as authoritative in Scripture. Although Hebrews 11:35-38 alludes to historical events recorded in 2 Maccabees 6:18-7:42.

4. Matthew 23:35 ~ Jesus implied that the close of Old Testament historical Scripture was the death of Zechariah (400 B.C.). This excludes any books written after Malachi and before the New Testament.

Other Disputed Books

There were other books that some people claimed to be Scripture. Some of them were written in the intertestamental period and called Old Testament pseudepigrapha (false writings). Others were written after the apostolic age (second-century A.D. and following). These are called New Testament pseudepigrapha. The writers often ascribed these books to the first-century apostles (*Gospel of Thomas* and the *Gospel of Peter*, etc.). They include some fanciful stories of Jesus' childhood and some heretical doctrines. No orthodox Christian seriously considered them to be inspired.

There was some other more sincerely written books that had devotional value and reveal some of the insights of Christian leaders after the first-century (*Shepherd of Hermas*, *Didache*, etc.). They are valuable historically, and even spiritually helpful but they do not measure up to the standards of canonicity and were not recognized as Scripture.

Formation

The formation of the New Testament canon began in the early part of the second-century A.D. The earliest list was drawn up in Rome, in A.D. 140, by the heretic Marcion. Although his list was not authoritative, it did demonstrate that the idea of a New Testament canon was accepted at that time. The concept we have today of a completed Bible was formulated early in the history of the church. By the end of the second century, all but seven books (Hebrews, 2 and 3 John, 2 Peter, Jude, James, and Revelation) were recognized as apostolic. And by the end of the fourth-century, all twenty-seven books in our present canon were recognized by all the churches of the West. After the Damasine Council of Rome in A.D. 332 and the third Council of Carthage in A.D. 397, the question of the Canon was closed in the West. By the year A. D. 500 the whole Greek-speaking church had also accepted all the books of our present New Testament.

Who decided which books should be placed in the Bible?

The simple answer is that God decided which books should be in the canon. He was the final determiner. J. I. Packer writes, "The church no more gave us the New Testament canon than Sir Isaac Newton gave us the force of gravity. God gave us gravity, by his work of creation, and similarly he gave us the New Testament canon, by inspiring the individual books that make it up."[110]

---

[110] J. 1. Packer, *God Speaks To Man: Revelation and the Bible*, (Westminster Press, 1965), 81.

Canonizing and Collecting

A distinction needs to be made between canonizing and collecting. In one sense no man or council can pronounce a work canonical or scriptural. Yet man was responsible for collecting and preserving such works. F. F. Bruce writes:

> One thing must be emphatically stated. The New Testament books did not become authoritative for the Church because they were formally included in a canonical list; on the contrary, the Church included them in her canon because she already regarded them as divinely inspired, recognizing their innate worth and generally apostolic authority, direct or indirect. The first ecclesiastical councils to classify the canonical books were both held in North Africa-at Hippo Regius in 393 and at Carthage in 397-but what these councils did was not to impose something new upon the Christian communities but to codify what was already the general practice of these communities.[111]

Hence, the books we have as Scripture were inspired by God and recognized as such by man.

We have begun to consider what criteria were used in determining which books belong in the Bible? The books admitted to the canon of Scripture were deemed to be inspired by God. Other books were deemed unworthy of inclusion. Why? There were many books that might have had some claim to inspiration. How did the people judge between the true and the false? The Bible itself does not give any set of criteria that ought to be used to determine which books were to be considered Scripture. Although we do not know the exact criteria which were used, they may include the following.

Prophetic Authorship

For a book to be considered canonical, it must have been written by a prophet or apostle or by one who had a special relationship with such (Mark to Peter, Luke to Paul). Only those who had witnessed the events or had recorded eyewitness testimony could have their writings considered as Holy Scripture.

---

[111] F. F. Bruce, *The New Testament Documents: Are They Reliable?* (Grand Rapids, Eerdmans, 1960), 27.

Witness of the Spirit

The appeal to the inner witness of the Holy Spirit was also made to aid the people in understanding which books belonged in the canon and which did not. Clark Pinnock writes:

> The Spirit did not reveal a list of inspired books, but left their recognition to a historical process in which He was active, God's people learned to distinguish wheat from chaff, and gold from gravel, as He worked in their hearts.[112]

Acceptance

The final test is the acceptance of the people of God. Jesus told His disciples, "But the Helper, the Holy Spirit, whom the Father will send in my name, he will teach you all things and bring to your remembrance all that I have said to you." (Jn. 14:26). We have the promise of Jesus that his disciples would be given total recall by the Holy Spirit of the things he said and did. These same disciples either wrote the New Testament books or had input into which works were accepted as Scripture. Any book that claimed canonical status, yet detracted from the truth of the life of Christ, would have been rejected by Jesus' own disciples who were eyewitnesses to the New Testament events. Thus the acceptance of God's people is an important criterion for a book to be considered canonical.

Nature of God

Another reason we can be assured the correct books are in the Bible is the nature of God. It has been estimated there are a quintillion (1 followed by 18 zeros) stars in the universe. The Bible says God calls them by their names. If God is able to do this, he certainly is able to preserve intact his Word for the benefit of mankind.

Jews and Protestants have the same Old Testament. The Old Testament consists of thirty-nine books according to the Protestant reckoning but only twenty-four according to the Jewish reckoning. The books are the same; the difference is in the way they are divided.

Protestant Bible

The division of the Protestant Bible is as follows:

- 17 historical books: Genesis --- Esther.

---

[112] Clark Pinnock, *Biblical Revelation*, (Grand Rapids: Baker, 1973), 104.

- 5 poetical books Job --- Song of Solomon.[113]

- 17 prophetical books: Isaiah-Malachi.

Hebrew division

The Hebrew Bible numbers these as twenty-four:

- The Torah or law contains five books, Genesis-Deuteronomy.

- The Prophets contain eight books, Joshua, Judges, Samuel, Kings, Isaiah, Jeremiah, Ezekiel, and the twelve minor prophets are grouped into one book.

- The Writings or *Kethubim* contain eleven books: Psalms, Proverbs, Song of Solomon, Ruth, Lamentations, Ecclesiastes, Esther, Daniel, Ezra-Nehemiah, and Chronicles.

- The Hebrew Bible combined 1 and 2 Samuel, 1 and 2 Kings, and 1 and 2 Chronicles.

- The twelve minor prophets were combined into one book.

Josephus numbered the books as twenty-two by attaching Ruth to Judges and Lamentations to Jeremiah. Thus, the books are identical. The only difference is in the way they are divided.

Council of Nicaea

There have been accusations that the Council of Nicaea had a tremendous effect on choosing what books should be in the Bible. It has also been suggested that this council changed some of the doctrines that the church held before that time. The Council of Nicaea met in A.D. 323 to discuss how Jesus Christ was related to God. There were some in the church, led by Arius of Alexandria, who denied that Jesus Christ was God in human flesh, the Second Person of the Trinity. In order to answer these issues, the church had to make a pronouncement on which books authoritative doctrine could be based on. The Council of Nicaea did not meet to discuss which books belonged in the New Testament canon. It only recognized the books that the church had from the beginning considered to be the Word of God.

Already composed

The books that were recognized as Scripture had already been composed at the time. All the books contained in the New Testament

---

[113] Some of these poetical books have been variously described/defined as "Wisdom" books.

were composed before the end of the first century. Some fifty existing papyrus manuscripts written before A.D. 325 contain parts of every book of the New Testament, except 1 Timothy. There is no truth to the argument, so often brought up, that some of these books were not in existence until the Council of Nicaea. The argument, therefore, that certain doctrine were invented at this time has no basis in fact.

Other early writings

There are some very early works in the history of the church that add to our information about Jesus. These books written between A.D. 80 and A.D. 180 were composed by "apostolic fathers." They were not inspired, as the New Testament, books are but they do provide us with some confirming information regarding the New Testament events. Some of the most notable examples include the following.

Letter of Clement

In A.D. 95, Clement of Rome wrote a letter to the Corinthian church. This is an extremely important work because Clement was the leading elder of the church at Rome. He wrote his letter to the Corinthians to end a dispute between the laity and the elders.[114]

Ignatius of Antioch

Ignatius of Antioch wrote seven letters in A.D. 115 on his way to being thrown to the lions. He made the distinction between his writings and that of the apostles, "I do not enjoin you as Peter and Paul did. They were apostles; I am a convict; they were free, but I am a slave to this very hour." (Ignatius, *Letter to the Romans*, 4.3).

Quadratus

Quadratus was one of the earliest defenders of the Christian faith. He wrote to Emperor Hadrian about A.D. 125. The work has been lost except for a brief statement in the writing of the church historian Eusebius. Quadratus gives another account of the miracles of Jesus and testifies as the Apostle Paul does that many who participated in the miraculous events surrounding the life of Christ lived long after Jesus ascended into heaven.

---

[114] The phrase "laity and elders" really belongs to particular theological interpretations rooted in ecclesiologies that are essentially hierarchical. Many Christians believe in the priesthood of all believers (1 Pet. 2:9). They do not argue so much that there ought to be no clergy, rather that there is no laity.

The Epistle of Barnabas

The Epistle of Barnabas (not the Barnabas of the New Testament), was written between A.D. 130 and 138. It was written to show that Jesus is a fulfillment of the Old Testament Law.

Though these books were written at an early date, they have never been seriously considered as Scripture. They do not claim biblical authority; some actually disclaim it. In addition, none of them were written by apostles or members of the apostolic company. But they are helpful in shedding light on the New Testament.

Why was the authority of certain Old Testament books questioned?

At certain times, some of the biblical books had their authority questioned. These include:

Esther

The problem with the Book of Esther is that the God is not mentioned in the book. The hand of God, however, is certainly evident in the story as he protected the Jews from total annihilation. The mere absence of God's name is not sufficient reason to deny its status, especially when his providential hand is so evident.

Ecclesiastes

Ecclesiastes was sometimes objected to because of its skeptical tone. The writer of the book exclaims. "Vanity of vanity, all is vanity" (Eccles. 1:2). The problem here is a matter of understanding the author's intent. Solomon, the writer of the book, is demonstrating that no one can experience ultimate satisfaction in this world. He shows that all people need God.

Song of Solomon

The Song of Solomon was sometimes criticized as being too sensual. The misdirected criticisms of sensuality do not understand the purpose of the book, which is to emphasize the nobility of marriage.

Ezekiel

There were some who considered the book of Ezekiel to be against the Mosaic Law. The problem was again one of interpretation, not inspiration.

Proverbs

Proverbs had some who doubted it because of certain supposed inner contradictions.

Yet a proper interpretation of the book will show this is not the case.

Why was the authority of certain New Testament books questioned?

Some of the books that are now in the New Testament canon have, at times, had their inspiration questioned. They are known as the *antilegomena*, "the books spoken against." Antilegomena, a direct transliteration from the Greek αντιλεγόμενα, refers to written texts whose authenticity or value is disputed. There were seven books whose authority was doubted by some members of the early church. The reasons vary from book to book. They are: -

Hebrews

The main problem that some of the early church members had with the book of Hebrews was that it was written anonymously. Yet Hebrews is not the only anonymous New Testament book. The four Gospels, for instance, do not name their authors either ~ though this is a convention of Gospel writing. From the earliest times, the letter to the Hebrews was accepted everywhere except in Latin Christianity. The problem still was a lack of a stated author. However, it was soon realized that Hebrews was orthodox in its content and deserved a place in the New Testament.

James

The main problem some had with James was the content. James put more emphasis on the obligation of believers to perform good works than do the other New Testament writings. But James is about the practical outworking and application of theological truth. It fits a much-needed gap between the doctrine and duty of Christianity.

Second Peter

The most suspect of all the books is 2 Peter. Basically, the reasons for questioning its authorship are the stylistic differences between it and 1 Peter. However, these stylistic differences can be explained by Peter's use of *amanuensis* (a scribe or secretary, to do the writing for him).

Second and Third John

Second and Third John were questioned for several reasons. First, the author was not specifically stated ~ he is called merely "the elder." Both of the letters were addressed to individuals, both are very brief, and were deemed by some to be without much theological content. Because of these factors, there were not too many early writers, who would quote from them.

Jude

Jude is a brief letter that gained immediate acceptance everywhere except Parthia, modern-day Iran. Jude was questioned for his use of the apocryphal book of Enoch.

Revelation

It is no surprise that the Book of Revelation would meet some opposition due to the apocalyptic and symbolic nature of the work. However, it had almost instant recognition everywhere except in Parthia. The biblical scholar R. H. Charles wrote concerning the Book of Revelation, "Throughout the Christian church during the second century, there is hardly any other book in the New Testament so well received as Revelation."[115]

We must remember that Jesus promised his disciples would be guided into all truth. These seven books were only questioned by some of the church, not all of it. They were eventually recognized by the whole church to be included in the New Testament canon.

Apocrypha

There is a group of writings which are considered part of Old Testament Scripture by the Roman Catholic Church. But these are not accepted as inspired by the Protestant church and Judaism. These are known as the Apocrypha. The word Apocrypha means "hidden" (ἀπόκρυφος, apókruphos). The Apocrypha refers to the fifteen books written between the years 300 BC and 100 BC (except Esdras which was written about A.D. 100). The number is fourteen if the Letter of Jeremiah is put with Baruch. Eleven of these fourteen books are considered to be sacred Scripture by the Roman Catholic Church. When added to the Old Testament they constitute only seven extra books because the others are attached to existing books. The Apocrypha is about the size of the New Testament.

Apocrypha and Apocryphal

Sometimes people confuse the terms Apocrypha and apocryphal. The word Apocrypha is a specific term used to refer to the particular books that are considered Scripture by the Roman Catholic Church. The term apocryphal is applied to other books that are New Testament forgeries. An example of this would be the *Gospel of Thomas*, which

---

[115] R. H. Charles, *Revelation*, *The International Critical Commentary*, Vol. 1, (Edinburgh: T & T Clark, 1906).

claims to have been written by Jesus' disciple Thomas. The book is a forgery.

History

The Protestant reformers, particularly in the sixteenth century, pointed out many cases of abuse in the Roman Catholic Church at that time. From 1545 to 1563, a church council met at Trent to answer some of their charges. Among their decisions was the pronouncement of these books as Holy Scripture. Before that time they were not regarded by the Roman Catholic Church as sacred Scripture. The Protestant church rejects them for the following reasons.

No claim

The primary reason for rejecting the Apocrypha as Scripture is that there is no claim within the books that they are inspired by God. This is in contrast to the canonical Scriptures, which claim to record the revelation of God.

Never cited as authoritative Scripture

Though the New Testament cites directly or alludes to almost every book of the Old Testament as Scripture, it never cites the Apocrypha as being God's Word. If the people living in the first century considered the Apocrypha Scripture, we would certainly expect them to refer to it as such.

However, what are we to make of Jude's quotation from the intertestamental book of Enoch, "Now Enoch, the seventh from Adam, prophesied about these men saying, 'Behold, the Lord comes with ten thousands of His saints.'" Jude records a prophecy made by Enoch, who lived before the flood of Noah. Enoch predicted the coming of the Lord to judge wicked individuals. The Apostle Paul wrote of this same judgment. (2 Thess. 1:7-10) This prophecy made by Enoch is not recorded in the Old Testament.

It is not necessary to assume that Jude considered the Book of Enoch as authoritative. Yes, the New Testament does refer to the Apocrypha in Jude 14 and Hebrews 11:35 but does not cite it as Holy Scripture. It cites the work in the same way Paul cited heathen poets (Acts 17:28).[116] This demonstrates that the New Testament writers were familiar with the Apocrypha but did not think of them as having the same status as Old Testament Scripture.

---

[116] Probably from Epimenides of Crete and Aratus' poem, *Phainomena* (Heavenly Displays).

Rejected by the Jews

The Jews have never considered these works to be inspired. On the contrary, they denied their inspiration. At the time of Christ we have the testimony of the Jewish writer Flavius Josephus that 22 books were deemed to be inspired by God (the reason for the number 22 rather than 39 is explained earlier). The books of the Apocrypha were not among these.

Not on early lists

In the early years of the church it drew up various lists of the books it considered to be Scripture. The books of the Apocrypha do not appear on any list until the fourth century.

Rejected by many Catholic scholars

Many Roman Catholic scholars, through the Protestant Reformation, rejected the Apocrypha as Scripture. There was no unanimity of opinion among them that these books should be considered Scripture.

Demonstrable errors

The Apocrypha also contains demonstrable errors. For example, Tobit was supposedly alive when Jeroboam staged his revolt in 931 B.C. and was still alive when the Assyrians captured the Northern kingdom of Israel in 721 B.C. This means that he lived over two hundred years. However, the Book of Tobit says he lived only 158 years (Tobit 1:3-5; 14:11). So it is not the longevity itself, but the detail of the lifespan is contradicted. This is an obvious contradiction. Other examples could be cited. Those who believe in an inerrant Scripture cannot accept the Apocrypha as God's Word.

No evidence of inspiration

The books of the Apocrypha do not contain anything like predictive prophecy that would give evidence of their inspiration. If these books were inspired by God, then we should expect to see some internal evidence confirming it. But there is none.

The Old Testament is complete

It is clear that in the first century the Old Testament was complete. The Hebrews accepted the same thirty-nine books, (although divided differently) that the Protestant church accepts today. Jesus put his stamp of approval on these books but said nothing concerning the Apocrypha. However, he did say that the Scriptures were the authoritative Word of God and could not be broken. Any adding to that which God has revealed is denounced in the strongest of terms. Therefore, we have the testimony of Jesus against the authenticity of the Apocrypha. The Apocrypha cannot be considered canonical because the books do not demonstrate themselves to be worthy of any claim to Scriptural status. Jesus did not consider it part of his Old Testament, and we are told not to add or subtract anything from God's Word.

What about other books that claim biblical authority?

Throughout the history of the church, many documents surfaced that claimed to have been written by the apostles or those intimately familiar with the life of Christ. However, these works were written by someone other than the named author. These fraudulent works are known as the *pseudepigrapha* (forgeries). They are also known as apocryphal works and were rejected by all. The early church father, Eusebius, called these books "totally absurd and impious." Over three hundred different works that fit into this category have been cataloged.

Other gospels

Among the forgeries were a large number of apocryphal or false gospels. Origen, a third-century writer, testified to the existence of other so-called gospels when he wrote, "There are many who have tried to write gospels, but not all have been accepted." The biblical scholar Edwin Yamauchi offers an appropriate comment:

> The apocryphal gospels are non-canonical writings of a motley variety about the purported deeds and revelations of Jesus Christ. Though the Greek word apocrypha originally meant "hidden," the church fathers used it to describe spurious writings foisted as gospels. Irenaeus refers to 'an unspeakable number of apocryphal and spurious writings, which they themselves (i.e. the heretics) had forged to bewilder the minds of the foolish.' Although some of them were patterned after the canonical gospels, many bear little resemblance to them. As Origen noted, 'The Church possesses four Gospels, heresy a great many.'[117]

Gnostic influence

Many of these works were influenced by Gnosticism. The word gnostic means "one who has knowledge." Gnosticism (from *gnostikos*, "learned," from Ancient Greek: γνῶσις *gnōsis*, knowledge). It is essentially a belief that the material world should be shunned, and the spiritual world should be embraced. The Gnostics taught that salvation

---

[117] Edwin M. Yamauchi, "The Word From Nag Hammadi," (*Christianity Today*, January 13, 1978), 19.

came by secret knowledge of God. The gnostic view of God is contrary to the Bible. In addition, the Gnostics considered that all matter is evil.

An example of gnostic writing can be found in the *Gospel of Philip*. The original *Gospel of Philip* was probably written sometime during the second century A.D. The influence of Gnosticism and its emphasis on secret knowledge can be clearly seen in this work:

> The Logos said: If you know the truth the truth will make you free. Ignorance is a slave, knowledge is freedom. When we recognize the truth we shall find the fruits of truth in our hearts. If we unite with it, we will bring our fulfillment.

Different level

Other statements show that they are on a different level than Scripture:

> A Gentile man does not die, for he has never lived that he should die. Adam came into being from two virgins, from the Spirit and from the virgin earth. Because of this Christ was born of a virgin, in order that he might set in order the stumbling which came to pass at the beginning.

These fanciful statements betray their non-biblical source.

Second-hand sources

The pseudepigrapha, apart from being forgeries, were also written long after, in some cases hundreds of years after, the New Testament events. The writers were not eyewitnesses to the life of Christ or to the events of the early church. This is another reason to reject the testimony which they give.

Gospel of Thomas

One of the most prominent of all the forgeries is the *Gospel of Thomas*. This was probably composed in Edessa in Syria about A.D. 140. Consisting of 114 sayings of Jesus, it is the most extensive collection of non-biblical sayings of Jesus that still exist. The Gospel of Thomas begins as follows, "These are the secret words which the living Jesus spoke, and Didymus Judas Thomas wrote. And He said: Whosoever finds the explanation of these words shall not taste death." We know that the *Gospel of Thomas* is a forgery for the following reasons.

Incorrect name

The author is not Thomas. Whoever wrote the *Gospel of Thomas* used the incorrect name when referring to the Apostle Thomas as Didymus Judas Thomas. In the four Gospels, Thomas is referred to as either Didymus or Thomas, not both at once. Didymus is the word for "twin" in both Greek and Aramaic. So the author of the *Gospel of Thomas* must not have been aware of this linguistic connotation.

Secret approach

The secret approach found in the *Gospel of Thomas* is typical of the writings of the Gnostics. The four Gospels are open about the ways of salvation and the kingdom of God while the *Gospel of Thomas* views truth from a hidden vantage point. There is no historical setting for the statements. The *Gospel of Thomas* is a compilation of sayings without the inclusion of important historical events as recorded in the Gospels. We are not told when or under what circumstances the statements were made.

Contradicts the four gospels

Many of the sayings are contradictory to those we have in the gospels. For example, saying 114:

> Jesus said, "See, I shall lead her, so that I will make her male, that she too may become a living spirit, resembling you males. For every woman who makes herself male will enter the Kingdom of Heaven."

Different Jesus

The person of Jesus Christ is different than the one revealed in the canonical gospels, where Jesus is God the Son, second person of the trinity. In the *Gospel of Thomas*, he is one who points the way by which an individual can attain the knowledge of God. These reasons demonstrate that the *Gospel of Thomas* is a forgery rather than a legitimate work written by one of Jesus' apostles.

Aquarian Gospel of Jesus Christ

One alternative explanation of the life and ministry of Jesus that has caused considerable interest is *The Aquarian Age Gospel of Jesus, the Christ of the Piscean Age*. This is a book by Levi H. Dowling, first published in 1908. He said he had transcribed the text of the book from the *Akashic* records. This is a compendium of mystical knowledge supposedly encoded in a non-physical plane of existence. The word *akashic* from *akasha* is a Sanskrit word meaning "sky" or "space." The *akashic* records are described as containing all knowledge of human experience as well as the history of the cosmos encoded in the very fabric of all existence. In the later twentieth-century, it was adopted by New Age, spiritual groups. The title is derived from the practice of astrology of naming time periods in terms of constellations and their dominant positions in the sky. This work written by Dowling (1844-1911) is allegedly based upon communication he received from a "universal mind."

The *Aquarian Gospel* attempts to fill in some of the missing years of Jesus' youth. It also tries to explain his wisdom by attributing it to contact with holy men of other religions. The astrological idea that a new Aquarian age has come upon us brings with it the need for a new spiritual gospel, the *Aquarian Gospel*.

Content

Some of the material in the *Aquarian Gospel* is borrowed from the ancient *Gospel of James*, a well-known forgery in the early years of the church. The most prominent part of the book deals with the education and travel of Jesus. According to the *Aquarian Gospel*, Jesus first studied under the Jewish teacher Hillel and then went to India to spend time with their holy men. His learning also supposedly took him to Tibet, Persia, Assyria, Greece, and Egypt. It was in Egypt that Jesus was said to have joined the sacred brotherhood. He passed through seven degrees and emerged as the Logos. In Alexandria, a council of seven sages was held where they ordained Jesus for the work of the ministry

The *Aquarian Gospel* then rewrites the four gospels according to its own particular viewpoint. The end of the story has Jesus appearing in a materialized body to people in India, Persia, Greece, and other countries.

Evaluation

Like many previous attempts, the *Aquarian Gospel* attempts to give an explanation of the wisdom and character of Jesus apart from the biblical depiction. Dowling's reconstruction shows obvious borrowing from the *Ancient Gospel of James*. It also shows familiarity with a nineteenth-century work, Nicolas Notovitch's *Unknown Life of Jesus Christ* (1887). Notovitch was a Russian aristocrat, Cossack officer, spy, and journalist. But he is best known for this book claiming that during his unknown years, Jesus left Galilee for India and studied with Buddhists and Hindus there before returning to Judea. Notovitch's claim was based on a document he said he had seen at the Hemis Monastery while he stayed there, but later confessed to having fabricated his evidence. Modern scholars view Notovitch's accounts of the travels of Jesus to India a hoax which includes major inconsistencies.

The book begins with a historical inaccuracy, "Augustus Caesar reigned, and Herod Antipas was ruler in Jerusalem." This is an error because Antipas ruled in Galilee, never in Jerusalem. A crucial problem with the *Aquarian Gospel* concerns its scenario of the source of Jesus' teachings. If Jesus obtained his wisdom from the masters of India, Greece, and other countries, then why doesn't his teaching reflect it? The teachings of Jesus, as recorded in the Gospels, are in direct conflict with every central belief of Hinduism, Buddhism, and the other religions with which he supposedly came into contact. The simple fact is that we have in the gospels a first-hand account of the life and ministry of Jesus.

The *Aquarian Gospel* is a false portrait of the life of Christ, not based upon historical records or eyewitness testimony but rather upon the recollections of an ancient forgery and the imagination of a twentieth-century writer. It has no value whatsoever in providing new or accurate information on the life of Christ.

The Archko Volume

One of the most famous written hoaxes is the *Archko Volume*. The work is also known as the *Report of Pilate* or *Archko Library*. The content of this work is an alleged report of the trial and death of Jesus made by Pontius Pilate to Emperor Tiberius. Its existence can be traced back to Rev. W. D. Mahan of Boonville, Missouri. He published a thirty-two-page pamphlet in 1879 entitled, "A Correct Transcript of Pilate's Court." The success of the *Report of Pilate* led Mahan to make some more "discoveries." These included:

- An interview with the shepherds who were given the announcement of Christ's birth.

- Gamaliel's interview with Joseph and Mary.

- Eli's story of the Magi, and other previously unknown interviews surrounding the life and ministry of Jesus.

Mahan claimed these "interviews" were translated from ancient manuscripts in Rome or Constantinople. Edgar Goodspeed writes concerning the accuracy of these:

> The picture of Jesus in his interview with Pilate is romantic and theatrical, and the Pilate reflected in the "Report" is historically improbable. The whole work is a weak, crude fancy, a jumble of high-sounding but meaningless words, and hardly worth serious criticism. It is difficult to see how it could have deceived anyone.... Like the "Report of Pilate," these [the other interviews] bristle with childish blunders...The supposed references to Josephus's *Jewish Wars*...simply do not exist. The statement that Josephus in his *Antiquities* refers to Jesus in more than fifty places is false...That Tacitus wrote his history of Agricola in A.D. 56 is of course an error; Tacitus was born in 55, and even if he had been able to write his father-in-law's

biography at the age of one year, there was nothing yet to write, for Agricola himself was only nineteen.[118]

As can be imagined, the *Report of Pilate* and the later interviews were immediately exposed as frauds. It was noticed, for instance, that entire pages of Eli's story of the Magi were copied verbatim from the novel *Ben Hur!* Unhappily, people continue to read and believe these fraudulent works although they have no basis in fact.

The Lost Books of the Bible

One of the most frequently asked questions concerns the so-called *Lost Books of the Bible*. A book with this title was produced in 1926. It was the reprint of William Hone's *Apocryphal New Testament*, first printed in 1820. Hone's book was copied from two earlier ones published in 1736 and 1737. Since the time of the original writing of the lost books, the field of manuscript studies has made tremendous advances. But none of this has been taken into account by those who publish these works. The contents of the *Lost Books* include the following:

Four Infancy Gospels

- *The Birth of Mary*, a work written in the middle of the second century.

- *The Protoevangelium of James* written about the same time.

- The first *Gospel of Infancy* composed about A.D. 400.

- *The Second Infancy Gospel*, which in reality is a fragment of the *Gospel of Thomas*.

These were so-called infancy gospels that were written to fill in the details of the early unrecorded years of the life of Christ. These works include stories of Jesus forming clay figures of animals and birds which he makes walk, fly, and eat. Another account has a child who runs into Jesus and falls down dead. These examples are representative of the fanciful nature of the accounts.

The Letter of King Abgar

This was supposedly a letter written to Jesus by Abgar, King of Edessa. Jesus' alleged reply to the letter is also contained. These works were written in the third century.

---

[118] Edgar Goodspeed, *Modern Apocrypha: Famous "Biblical" Hoaxes*, Beacon Press, 1956), 33, 35.

Gospel of Nicodemus

This is also known as *The Acts of Pilate*. It was written in the fourth or fifth century. Other works found among the lost books include the *Apostles' Creed*. And the spurious letter from Paul to the Laodiceans. These books have been called "outlaw" Scriptures by some. But none of these works were ever thought of as part of the New Testament. Anyone who claims these works were suppressed by the church is speaking out of ignorance or a desire to deceive. It is obvious from the date of composition of these works that they cannot be considered authoritative. The New Testament was written by eyewitnesses or people who recorded eyewitness testimony of the life and ministry of Jesus.

Contrast with the four gospels

F.W. Farrar wrote:

> The Four Gospels superseded all others and won their way into universal acceptance by their intrinsic value and authority. After so many salutary losses we still possess a rich collection of Apocryphal Gospels, and, if they serve no other good purpose, they have this value, that they prove for us undoubtedly the unique and transcendent superiority of the sacred records. These bear the stamp of absolute truthfulness, all the more decisively when placed in contrast with the writings which show signs of willful falsity. We escape their lying magic to find support and help from the genuine gospels. And here we take refuge with the greater confidence because the ruins which lie around the ancient archives of the Church look like a guarantee of the enduring strength and greatness of those archives themselves.[119]

Has God revealed anything further to mankind since the first century?

The mere claim that God spoke to an individual does not make it true. There has to be evidence to back up the claim. Does the evidence support the claim that God spoke through them? The Bible instructs us to test the spirits, "Beloved, do not believe every spirit, but test the spirits whether they are of God; because many false prophets have gone out into the world." (1 Jn. 4:1).When we test the claims of those who have brought forth a "new Scripture" we find them to be untrue.

The downfall of all the books that have had inspiration claimed for them is that they present a different revelation from what has previously been recorded. They contradict the Bible. For example, the *Quran* says

---

[119] F. W. Farrar, *The Messages of the Books*, (Nabu Press, 2010), 27.

that Jesus was not the Son of God and that he did not die on the cross for the sins of the world. The sacred books of Mormonism teach that there exist many gods rather than the one God of the Bible. In addition, Mormonism teaches that each male can someday become a god himself. Mormonism thus denies the doctrine of the Trinity. It denies salvation by grace through faith and the eternal punishment of the wicked. Every book written since the completion of the Bible that claims to be a further revelation from God fails on the same ground. They all deny that Jesus Christ is God, the second person of the trinity. These works also deny salvation by grace through faith. They preach a different gospel. The Apostle Paul warned the church at Galatia about such people, "I marvel that you are turning away so soon from Him who called you in the grace of Christ, to a different gospel...But even if we, or an angel from heaven, preach any other gospel to you than what we have preached to you, let him be accursed."—Galatians 1:6, 8.

Furthermore, there is no substantiating evidence (such as fulfilled prophecy) to demonstrate the books are of divine inspiration. The various books that have been written since the completion of the New Testament, that have claimed to be a further revelation from God, fall short of the mark. The Bible warns, "Every word of God is pure; he is a shield to those who put their trust in him. Do not add to his words, lest he reprove you and you be found a liar."—Proverbs 30:5-6.

Nothing can be added to the Bible

The canon was closed in the first century. Since then God has not revealed anything on the same level with Scripture.

Westminster Confession

The Westminster Confession, a seventeenth-century statement of faith, says concerning the Bible:

> The whole counsel of God, concerning all things necessary for His own glory, man's salvation, faith and life, is either expressly set down in Scripture, or by good and necessary consequence may be deduced from Scripture: unto which nothing at any time is to be added, whether by new revelations of the Spirit, or traditions of men (*Westminster Confession*, 1:6).

This statement sums up the Protestant view of Scripture. Nothing is to be added or subtracted from the Bible. The revelation from God to man has been completed. However, there is no direct word in the Bible that says God has stopped revealing himself.

Some have appealed to the following verses in the Book of Revelation, "For I testify to everyone who hears the words of the prophecy of this book: If anyone adds to these things, God will add to him the plagues that are written in this book; and if anyone takes away from the words of the book of this prophecy, God shall take away his part from the Book of Life." (Rev. 22:18, 19). This is only speaking of the Book of Revelation. It is not a commandment against adding any other book to Scripture. If taken literally, then you could not have any other book in Scripture but the Book of Revelation!

Yet there is a principle here that is clearly taught. No one is to add or to take away from the revealed Word of God. Jude makes a statement that is pertinent to our discussion, "I found it necessary to write to you exhorting you to contend earnestly for the faith which was once for all delivered to the saints." (Jude 3). This verse teaches that a body of truth from God has been delivered to man and that this faith has been wholly delivered. This seems to indicate that no further revelation from God is necessary. God has told us in Scripture everything that we need to know about who he is, who we are, and what will happen to the earth in the future.

APPENDIX 1 Does God Change His Mind?

How this question is answered has a bearing on our understanding of the doctrine of God, particularly in relation to aspects of his character such as his sovereignty and immutability. But it also affects our understanding of prayer. Can God be persuaded or prevailed upon in prayer to acquiesce to our persistent pleas? Some would say "yes" and suggest that this is the point of the Parable of the Persistent Widow where Jesus told his disciples they "ought always to pray and not lose heart" (Lk. 18:1).

The Case of Sodom

One might argue that there are instances recounted in Scripture where God was prevailed upon to change his mind. For example, the occasion when God threatened to destroy Sodom and all its inhabitants, but Abraham pleaded with God to spare the city if it had just ten righteous inhabitants. In that narrative, Abraham is bargaining with God. But in doing so he learns something of the merciful nature of the Almighty; that the Lord is "not wishing that any should perish, but that all should reach repentance." (2 Pet. 3:9).

The Case of Hezekiah

> In those days, Hezekiah became sick and was at the point of death. And Isaiah the prophet the son of Amoz came to him, and said to him, "Thus says the LORD: Set your house in order, for you shall die, you shall not recover." Then Hezekiah turned his face to the wall and prayed to the LORD, and said, "Please, O LORD, remember how I have walked before you in faithfulness and with a whole heart, and have done what is good in your sight." And Hezekiah wept bitterly. Then the word of the LORD came to Isaiah: "Go and say to Hezekiah, 'Thus says the LORD, the God of David your father: I have heard your prayer; I have seen your tears. Behold, I will add fifteen years to your life.'"—Isaiah 38:1-5.

Did God change his mind? God cannot change his mind without contradicting his unchanging nature. God intended all along to heal Hezekiah. Withholding that news from Hezekiah stimulated him to pray intensely. Hezekiah did not change God's mind. But prayer helped Hezekiah discover God's purpose so he could align his life and actions to it. Hezekiah availed of the grace that was always available to him through prayer.

A sovereign God can predetermine to change his course of action in response to our prayers. His ultimate purposes are, therefore, unchangeable. He builds options into his purposes from the start. There is flexibility in the outcome to accommodate the various responses of people. God is something like a traveler who plans a destination but allows freedom to change the route or make spontaneous side trips along the way. Thus, God's will is dynamic.

We might compare the relationship between God, his will and his people to a chess match between a novice player and a master. The novice can make any move he chooses, and the master will respond accordingly. But the master will always be in control of the game.

God the Unchangeable

Malachi records the words of God on this matter: "I the LORD do not change" (Mal. 3:6). The book of Numbers also comments on this issue: "God is not man, that he should lie, or a son of man, that he should change his mind" (Num. 23:19). In the New Testament God's immutability is asserted where James speaks of the Lord "with whom there is no variation or shadow due to change" (Jas. 1:17). These verses assert that God is not only unchanging, but he is unchangeable. As the great hymn in praise of God's faithfulness proclaims, "There is no shadow of turning with Thee."

How then, might verses such as Genesis 6:6 be understood and explained? There we read that "the LORD was sorry that he had made man on the earth, and it grieved him to his heart." This verse declares that God regretted creating man. Obviously, he did not reverse his decision. Instead, through Noah, he allowed man to continue to exist. The fact that we are alive today is proof that God did not change his mind about creating man. In addition, the context of this passage is a description of the sinful state in which man was living, and it is man's sinfulness that triggered God's sorrow, not man's existence.

The Case of Nineveh

Speaking of the Ninevites Jonah 3:10 says, "When God saw what they did, how they turned from their evil way, God relented of the disaster that he had said he would do to them, and he did not do it." Similarly, in Exodus (in relation to the incident concerning the golden calf and the idolatry and debauchery of God's people) Moses pleaded with

God to avert his anger. It is recorded that "the LORD relented from the disaster that he had spoken of bringing on his people" (Ex. 32:14). Again, the same Hebrew word is used, which translates "to be sorry for." Why was God sorry for the Ninevites? Because they had a change of heart and as a result changed their ways from disobedience to obedience. He was going to judge Nineveh because of its evil. However, Nineveh repented and changed its ways. As a result, God had mercy on Nineveh, which is entirely consistent with his character.

In the book of Jonah, the response of God to the Ninevites presents the reader with a great contrast between the heart of Jonah and the heart of God (3:10-4:11). Jonah's heart is narrow, shriveled and constricted. God's heart is expansive, vast, and full to overflowing with mercy and grace. This contrast is set before us in the most vivid way. God bestows blessing, but Jonah begrudges this to the Ninevites. Obviously, he has forgotten; if he ever understood in the first place, not only that nobody deserves God's blessing but that everybody deserves death.

The Wrath of God

We should understand that the Ninevites avail of the mercy extended to them rather than thinking that God responded to their repentance. The phrase "God saw" (Jonah 3:10) does not merely refer to knowledge of what happened. It does not mean that God only became aware of it at that point. That is a human perspective, but the divine perspective is quite different. Neither does it refer exclusively to God's omniscience. Certainly, God knows all things and knows them before they occur, but the phrase "God saw" means, importantly, that he took it to heart. God is not a mere observer of their repentance. He was the author of it. He worked in their hearts! He took the initiative. So here is God beholding the fruit of his own mighty works, with delight!

Consider the Parables of the Lost Coin, The Lost Sheep and The Lost Son (the prodigal). In each case the "owner" of that which was lost overflows with joy when it is found (Lk. 15). Scripture informs us that there is joy in the presence of the angels when a sinner repents.

Romans 3:23 teaches that all men sin and fall short of God's standard and Romans 6:23 states that the consequence for this is death (spiritual and physical). So the people of Nineveh deserved punishment. It is man's sinful condition and sinful actions that separate him from God. It would be contrary to the character of God not to punish the Ninevites had they continued in sin. However, the people of Nineveh turned to obedience, and for that, the Lord chose not to punish them. Did the change on the part of the Ninevites obligate God to do what he did?

Absolutely not! God cannot be placed in a position of obligation to man. Had the Lord not preserved the Ninevites, it would have been contrary to his character.

God is Consistent

The Scriptures that are interpreted as God seeming to change his mind are human attempts to explain the actions of God. God always knows what he is going to do. God does what he needs to do to cause humanity to fulfill his perfect plan: "My counsel shall stand, and I will accomplish all my purpose...I have spoken, and I will bring it to pass; I have purposed, and I will do it" (Isa. 46:10-11). God threatened Nineveh with destruction, knowing that it would cause Nineveh to repent. At the foot of Mount Sinai God threatened Israel with destruction, knowing that Moses would intercede! God threatened Sodom with destruction knowing it was doomed. God does not change his mind but rather acts consistently with his Word.

Scripture teaches the concept of God's immutability (i.e., the notion that his essence, character, and will are stable and perfect). Thus, while people undergo transformation, the changeless creator does not. He is the same forever. With the Lord, there can be no variation (Jas. 1:17; Heb. 13:8). God is not uncertain, indecisive, capricious or whimsical.

The concept of omniscience suggests that the Lord knows everything there is to know ~ past, present, and future. He has never learned anything, nor has he discovered a new fact. He is never surprised by what people may do. He knows our thoughts (Heb. 4:12-13), and the very intricacies of our bodies (Ps. 139; Mt. 10:30). Not even a bird falls to the earth without his knowing it.—Matthew 10:29.

Figures of Speech

It is impossible to conclude that the creator of the universe (omnipotent, omniscient, immutable...) changes his mind in any literal sense. But Scripture frequently employs figures of speech that might (at a superficial level) seem to suggest that God alters his actions in response to man's behavior. The passage in Exodus 32 is an example of this sort of phraseology.

Following the golden calf incident and the intercession of Moses the biblical text records God's *response*: "the LORD relented from the disaster that he had spoken of bringing on his people" (Ex. 32:14).

The word "relented" is a figure of speech (anthropopathism, which literally means "man feelings"). This is an idiom by which divine activity is described symbolically in terms of human emotion. It is similar to the kindred figure, anthropomorphism (which literally means "man form") by which God is described as having physical parts (e.g., eyes, hands, etc.) even though he is not a physical being (John 4:24; Luke 24:39). Anthropopathism, therefore, is a figure of speech by which human feelings or emotions are ascribed to God, in order to accommodate man's ignorance of the unfathomable intentions and operations of the deity (Rom. 11:33-36). Alan Cole explains that anthropopathism is a figure of speech used in Exodus:

> ...by which God's activity is explained, by analogy, in strictly human terms. The meaning is not that God changed His mind; still less that He regretted something that He had intended to do. It means, in biblical language, that He now embarked on a different course of action from that already suggested as a possibility, owing to some new factor which is usually mentioned in the context. In the Bible, it is clear that God's promises and warnings are always conditional on man's response: this is most clearly set out in Ezekiel 33:13-16. We are not to think of Moses as altering God's purpose towards Israel by his prayer, but as carrying it out: Moses was never more like God than in such moments, for he shared God's mind and loving purpose.[120]

The notion of contingency (hinging as it does on the word "if") helps us to understand that though certain biblical passages speak of the Lord being changeless and others seem to represent him as changing (in response to human conduct) that there is no contradiction here.

It is important to understand some of the common figures of speech utilized by the Bible writers, under the guiding influence of the Holy Spirit in order to avoid making faulty conclusions ~ sometimes very dangerous ones. Hence there is a need for hermeneutics (the principles of biblical interpretation) to avoid exegetical fallacies, flawed theology and inappropriate application of the Word.

Helpful Insight

So what does Scripture mean when it states that God relented? It does not mean that he changed his mind. The book of Jeremiah contains a helpful insight into this issue:

---

[120] Alan Cole, *Exodus, Tyndale Old Testament Commentaries*, (Downers Grove, IL: InterVarsity, 1973), 217.

If at any time I declare concerning a nation or a kingdom, that I will pluck up and break down and destroy it, and if that nation, concerning which I have spoken, turns from its evil, I will relent of the disaster that I intended to do to it. And if at any time I declare concerning a nation or a kingdom that I will build and plant it, and if it does evil in my sight, not listening to my voice, then I will relent of the good that I had intended to do to it.—Jeremiah 18:7-10.

Nineveh is a classic example of the teaching of Jeremiah 18. There is a living interaction between God and the Ninevites. Their sin is precipitating judgment, but God is saying if this condition changes his response will be different.

This does not in any way invalidate the fixed decrees and sovereign purposes of God. Judgment is contingent upon certain realities. The revealed activity of God is the only valid commentary on the character and purposes of God. Scripture shows his redemptive plans unfolding throughout history. The pulse of chapter 4 of Jonah throbs to the rhythm of God's gracious heart. He takes no sadistic pleasure in judgment. God never brings judgment until the cup of iniquity is so full that to allow it to go unpunished would be a contradiction of his moral character. Even then he does it with some measure of reluctance. The sovereign, eternal, omnipotent God of the Bible is a living God, not a detached, distant and aloof God of fate.

A False Picture of God

Much of the production of goods today is automated. There are computerized systems where certain buttons are pushed, and it is impersonal; a machine produces the end product. Whatever was decreed by the computer program will be the outcome. This is how some people understand God. However, this is a false picture of God. It is not that somewhere in the distant past God fed everything into the program and has pushed certain buttons and now sits back and watches it all unfold and makes sure there are no breakdowns or short circuits in the system and if there are he will mend them. The God of the Bible is not detached from the outworking of the details of our lives. Scripture emphasizes the intimate, sensitive involvement of the living, personal God with his people.

Some people are very reluctant to let go of the notion that God can be prevailed upon (through prayer) to change his mind. I am not just referring to young, immature believers. The same could be said of some leaders in the church and even some preachers. Separating people from their cherished beliefs is as difficult as taking candy from a baby (whoever said that was easy must have had a very different experience of children to that which most people know to be true).

Why pray?

So why bother praying at all? Prayer does not change God's mind but it ought to have the effect of bringing our minds into alignment with his. It ought to change our hearts in terms of our desires and influence our motives. Prayer should bring our wayward wills into harmony with God's will. Engaging in prayer is a vital exercise in our sanctification inasmuch as it assists in the ongoing process of our transformation into the likeness of Jesus. Christ is our constant companion, and he does not change, Jesus Christ is the same yesterday and today and forever.' (Heb. 13:8) We can rest in that constancy with confidence.

APPENDIX 2 The Trial of Jesus[121]

Jesus had just observed the Passover with his disciples. He instituted what is now known as the Lord's Table. He agonized in the garden of Gethsemane. There we witness the struggle of Jesus and how he acted under pressure. We see his absolute surrender to the will of the heavenly Father. Judas Iscariot betrayed Jesus with a kiss and Christ was arrested. Much had happened but more was about to unfold. Here is an account of the Lord's trial before the Sanhedrin. In this trial, Jesus is accused and condemned by the very people he came to this world to save. They are in the presence of the promised Messiah but they do not recognize him, acknowledge him or submit to him. The account in John's Gospel reveals that Jesus was first taken to the home of Annas. (Jn. 18:13) He was the father-in-law of the High Priest Caiaphas and a man of considerable influence. When Annas finished questioning Jesus, he sent him, bound, to Caiaphas.—John 18:24.

The text deals with the Lord's trial before the Sanhedrin. This council was the seventy member supreme court of Israel. The word "Sanhedrin" literally means, "to sit together." They were the official rulers of the nation. The members of this body were chosen for their maturity and wisdom. They were expected to be fair and impartial in all their rulings. The High Priest was in charge of the proceedings. These people were already convinced of Jesus' guilt. They merely went through the motions of securing evidence against him. They behaved like prosecutors rather than independent and impartial arbiters of justice.

The Trial Was Illegal

However, this was an illegal trial. It was illegal because of *when* it was held. Under Judaic laws, which regulated the court system, a trial at night was prohibited. Luke's account says "daybreak." But that must refer to the second trial as other Gospel accounts put it at night. This is corroborated by Peter's denials which were before the cock crowed at daybreak. It was also illegal to hold a trial on a feast day and this was the Passover feast. Having a trial at such a time might prevent the entire council from gathering. And it would prevent the accused from mounting an effective defense as it would make it more difficult for witnesses to come to the trial. So this trial obviously violated these regulations since it was held at night and on the Passover.

---

[121] This appendix is from Kieran Beville, *Journey with Jesus through the Message of Mark*, (Cambridge, Ohio, Christian Publishing House, 2015). Used here with permission.

This trial was rigged. The slightest inconsistency in the evidence of witnesses should have been enough to acquit Jesus. There were insufficient grounds to convict. Christ's condemnation was based on the testimony of false witnesses and erroneous accusations. This passage of Scripture reveals the true character and condition of the human heart. His trial took place at night but as soon as dawn begins to break, the Sanhedrin convened again to legitimize the illegal decisions they reached during the night.

However, it was also illegal because of *where* it was held. Jewish law mandated that all trials conducted by the Sanhedrin were to be held in The Hall of Hewn Stones. This was located in the temple grounds. This rule was violated because the preliminary trial was first held in the home of Annas. And then transferred to the private residence of the High Priest. (Lk. 22:54) The Sanhedrin was behaving more like a private club than a public body elected to oversee judicial proceedings in a fair manner. It was also illegal because of the *way* it was held. There are many problems with the trial of Jesus that night. Among the illegalities of his trial are the following:

- Trials were illegal on the eve of the Sabbath because Jewish law required a one day adjournment in the event of a conviction.

- A guilty sentence could only be handed down the day after a trial.

- The Sanhedrin could not bring charges against a defendant. They could only investigate charges that had been made by others.

- The charges against Jesus were changed during the trial. He was first charged with threatening to destroy the temple. Later, he was charged with blasphemy. Then, when he stood before Pilate, his charges were changed again. This time he was charged with claiming to be the King of the Jews and forbidding the paying of taxes to Rome.

- Jesus was not allowed a defense before the court.

- All charges against him should have been thoroughly investigated.

- And he should have been allowed time to call his own witnesses.

- The Sanhedrin pronounced the death sentence (v.64). But under the law, the Sanhedrin could not convict or pass down a death sentence. Under Roman rule, they could not execute the sentence of death. Their remit only allowed them to examine the prisoner and pass judgment. This had to be ratified by the Roman authorities

This trial was illegal because of *why* it was held. It was not about seeking the truth of a man's guilt or innocence. In the eyes of the Sanhedrin, Jesus was guilty before the trial ever began. He had no chance of leaving this trial with anything but a guilty verdict and a sentence of death. This trial was illegal because of *the witnesses* they called. The Jewish leaders have a problem. The men actually went out and sought witnesses to testify against Jesus (v.55). Effectively they recruited false witnesses, "...many bore false witness against him, but their testimony did not agree." (14:56). There were many who came forward that night willing to lie. They lied against the one who had done nothing but good and who had said nothing but the truth. Furthermore, their testimonies were inconsistent with one another. According to the law, the testimony of witnesses in a trial had to be in perfect agreement, "On the evidence of two witnesses or of three witnesses the one who is to die shall be put to death; a person shall not be put to death on the evidence of one witness." (Deut. 17:6). A couple of chapters later there is further comment, "A single witness shall not suffice against a person for any crime or for any wrong in connection with any offense that he has committed. Only on the evidence of two witnesses or of three witnesses shall a charge be established."—Deuteronomy 19:15.

Finally, some people informed the court that Jesus had threatened to destroy the temple and to build it again in three days. But again their versions of what Jesus said didn't agree (v.59). The word "temple" in (v.58) refers to the Holy Place, not the entire temple grounds. So they are accusing Jesus of threatening to demolish the holiest place in all of Israel. To their ears, it was utterly sacrilegious. Add to that the ludicrous claim that he would rebuild the temple in three days. When it had already been under construction for forty-six years and it is evident that such crass literalism in the interpretation of Christ's words regarding the temple was a convenient and cynical ploy to destroy him. Actually Jesus never said what they claimed he said. The Lord said, "Destroy this temple, and in three days I will raise it up." (Jn. 2:19). He was not referring to the temple in Jerusalem. He was referring to his own body that would be destroyed on the cross and raised from the dead three days later (Jn. 2:21). Jesus never said that he would destroy anything. At best, this accusation was based on a misunderstanding or misinterpretation of what Jesus said.

The Gospels make it clear that these were false accusations. It is astonishing that not a single person came forward in the Lord's defense that night. His accusers were not looking for his friends. They were looking for those who would testify against him. It is sad to think that there were some there who could have stood up for Jesus. Peter and

John were nearby. (Jn. 18:15) They were too afraid to come forward and speak up. If the Sanhedrin had searched they would have found many who could give favorable testimony about Jesus. People like:

- Lazarus

- former lepers

- a man who had been paralyzed but was restored to mobility

- Jairus and his daughter

- the widow of Nain and her son

- the Gadarene demoniac (now in his right mind)

- the woman who once had an issue of blood for twelve years

- and others

However, they were only interested in finding fault and ridding themselves of Jesus once and for all. It is amazing that with all the people Jesus had helped, ministered to, fed, healed, blessed and taught, no one stood with him on that terrible night. However, many were willing to put their lives on the line to falsely accuse Jesus:

> A single witness shall not suffice against a person for any crime or for any wrong in connection with any offense that he has committed. Only on the evidence of two witnesses or of three witnesses shall a charge be established. If a malicious witness arises to accuse a person of wrongdoing, then both parties to the dispute shall appear before the LORD, before the priests and the judges who are in office in those days. The judges shall inquire diligently, and if the witness is a false witness and has accused his brother falsely, then you shall do to him as he had meant to do to his brother. So you shall purge the evil from your midst.—Deuteronomy 19:16-19.

If a man was proven to be a false witness, he was to receive the same punishment that would have come to the man he lied against. Jesus stands alone among his enemies. These men did not care that Jesus was innocent. They hated him because he was a threat to their way of life and the power and status they had in society. They hated him so much that they were willing to lie, to break their own laws and to condemn an innocent man to death.

It is still the same today! Many religious institutions exercise power abusively. There are still people in our world who hate the name of Jesus so much that they will do anything in their power to discredit or destroy him and all those who follow him. Atheism is becoming more aggressive and secularism more militant. Jesus said: "If they persecuted me, they will also persecute you."—John 15:20.

As the trial continues, Caiaphas has a real problem. It is impossible to convict Jesus with the testimony of conflicting witnesses, so he changes tactics. He is frustrated with the proceedings thus far so he assumes the role of prosecutor and goes on the attack. He is mystified by the fact that Jesus has not opened his mouth to refute the lies the false witnesses have told about him. So he calls on Jesus to defend himself. In response to Caiaphas' demands, Jesus remains silent. Here Jesus fulfills the prophecy of Isaiah, "He was oppressed, and he was afflicted, yet he opened not his mouth." (Isa. 53:7). Caiaphas attempts to force Jesus to declare his deity. He is trying to get Jesus to incriminate himself on record. Caiaphas asks Jesus: "Are you the Christ, the Son of the Blessed?" Jesus does not disappoint Caiaphas. He answered, "I am..." He tells them that they judge him now but he will ultimately judge them. The Sanhedrin thought they were in control that night but they were terribly wrong. When Caiaphas hears these words of Jesus, he has heard all that he needs to hear.

Caiaphas rips his own clothes. This was a dramatic reaction to what he considered blasphemy.[122] It was a symbolic display designed to convey horror in the face of a terrible crime against God. In fact it is something he ought not to have done as it was expressly forbidden, "The priest who is chief among his brothers, on whose head the anointing oil is poured and who has been consecrated to wear the garments, shall not let the hair of his head hang loose nor tear his clothes." (Lev. 21:10). When Caiaphas ripped his garments, he (unintentionally) disqualified himself from the office of High Priest.

The one standing before him was qualified for that office as the great High Priest. What a contrast between the behavior of Caiaphas and the behavior of Christ! The whole council renders their guilty verdict. After Jesus is condemned the true nature of these men comes out. These educated, refined, religious leaders turn on Jesus like thugs. They spit in the Savior's face ~ though it is not overtly stated that the Sanhedrin were the ones who spat at Jesus and beat him. It is clear that the soldiers beat him but others did as well.

The Sanhedrin was central to the proceedings that night and if they did not *participate* in this violence they *permitted* it. They certainly had the power to stop it if they so desired. It is very likely that they were the very ones who engaged in this physical violence against the Lord. After all they were determined to kill him and plotted to murder him and carried

---

[122] Anyone who doubts that Jesus claimed to be God should take note.

out that wicked scheme under the cloak of justice. They had been frustrated in many such attempts up to now and here they most likely gave vent to those frustrations through violent action. But, it is the fulfillment of prophecy, "I gave my back to those who strike, and my cheeks to those who pull out the beard; I hid not my face from disgrace and spitting."—Isaiah 50:6.

Peter says, "When he was reviled, he did not revile in return; when he suffered, he did not threaten, but continued entrusting himself to him who judges justly." (1 Pet. 2:23) Jesus endured all this in order to redeem those who would turn to him in repentance and faith. Whether we know it or not everyone stands before Jesus in judgment. Like those religious Jews, people must decide whether they will believe him or reject him. What will you decide? When you see Jesus one day (and you will) will you see him as your Lord and Savior? Or, will you face him as your Judge? Will you embrace him in gratitude for the price he paid to redeem sinners? It is time for you to decide where you stand in regard to Jesus. Is he a liar or lunatic to be rejected? Or, is he to be loved and obeyed as Savior and Lord?

APPENDIX 3 The Pharisee and the Tax Collector

In the parable of The Pharisee and the Tax Collector (Lk. 18:9-14) we see two different kinds of men, two different approaches to God and two different outcomes. It is an ancient message, which demands modern application. It has to be taken out of the "then and there" and applied to the "here and now." It also needs to be taken out of the "THEM and there" and applied to "US and now."

This parable tells us something about the right and wrong way to approach God. The Pharisee is a religious man who is unaware of his need for mercy. He belonged to an elitist group of experts in Judaic law. They were the theologians of their day. As custodians of truth they corrupted it by adding man-made regulations which became burdensome traditions imposed on people. Pharisees were the strictest sect of the day. They took pride in their piety and privileged position. They were prejudiced against Gentiles and Hebrew sinners.

Unaware of His Unworthiness

We encounter this Pharisee praying in the temple but he seems completely unaware of his unworthiness. His greatest need is for mercy but he is ignorant of it as he prays about himself in what is an exercise in public self-congratulation. This man's approach to God contrasts with that of Isaiah, "Woe is me! For I am lost." (Isa. 6:5) Isaiah was acutely aware of his sinful condition in the presence of the holy God. However, this man recited the good things he does and the bad things he abstains from doing. His is a misplaced confidence in self-righteousness. God despises every manifestation of hypocrisy but rewards humility.

Sacrifice

If what the Pharisee said was true, there was some degree of sacrifice in his religious observance. He did not steal (he said) but was he not at that very moment robbing God of the honor due to him? He says he does not commit adultery, but Christ taught that to look at a woman with lust was adulterous. How pure can any man's heart be in this regard? He says he is not an evildoer, but Scripture teaches that all have sinned and fallen short of the glory of God. (Rom. 3:23) He says that he fasts twice a week and gives a tenth of all he gets. However, this sacrifice is offered to God in order to gain merit and so his approach is fatally flawed.

Sincerity

There is also a degree of sincerity in his religion but he is sincerely wrong in his approach to God. This is true of much religion today that is characterized by sacrifice and sincerity. He expresses contempt rather than concern for the tax collector. This lack of compassion is contrary to the heart of God. The Lord is: "merciful and gracious, slow to anger, and abounding in steadfast love and faithfulness, keeping steadfast love for thousands, forgiving iniquity and transgression and sin." (Ex. 34:6-7) The Pharisee compares himself, by contrast, to a sinful wretch. He did not compare himself to one of the great holy men of the Old Testament (even though they were all sinners) as this would have shown him in a less favorable light. His prayer was nothing more than a form of self-deception. We must beware that we do not engage in prayer in an unworthy manner.

Many people today console themselves that they are not as bad as so-and-so. He has had an affair but I have been faithful to my wife. He has stolen things from work but I have been honest. He does not go to church but I always attend Sunday services. He does not give money to charity but I am on the charity committee and I tithe a tenth. He drinks alcohol but I abstain. He smokes and uses coarse language but I abstain from these. What the Pharisee did and abstained from doing was appropriate but not as a package offered to God to earn merit toward justification. Isaiah says, "all our righteous acts are like filthy rags." (Isa. 64:6) This being so, what are our sins like?

True Standard

In weights and measures there are true standards by which we make judgments about the value of things, such as: 2 kilos of sugar, 1 acre of farm land or a square meter of carpet. Imagine carpeting your home by guessing the length and width of the rooms. It cannot be a matter of speculation. A measuring tape is required to identify precise dimensions. In evaluating our righteousness there is also a true standard; that standard is Jesus. There is no other standard. When measured against him we become conscious of our own unworthiness and our need of mercy. Our religion must be characterized by compassion for sinners and our concern should be evident in our prayers. In practice people need to feel welcome rather than labeled, despised, excluded and rejected. We are merely beggars telling other beggars where to find the bread of life.

Real Encounters with God

Real encounters with God are life transforming. They may not be dramatic, but they move us closer to the mind and heart of God. The Pharisee went to a good place; the temple and for a good reason, to pray. Many religious people today go to special buildings to pray but leave those places without having met with God. They are coming to God on their own terms seeking meritorious favor for their acts of righteousness and are ignorant of their greatest need, for mercy.

However, there is another man in this parable, a tax collector. First-century tax collectors in Palestine were generally ruthless, as one would have to be to collect tax for the Roman occupying power. Their work involved other unpleasant duties such as repossessions, evictions, and imprisoning poor defaulters. Many of them were extortionists who demanded more than was due, thus making their living by keeping the surplus. Many of them sub-contracted their duties to others and became rich by obtaining a percentage from each of their sub-contractors. Thus unfortunate debtors often had to pay exorbitant additions to what they owed. Contractors would frequently engage sub-contractors from the localities where debtors lived. This local information helped contractors but made the tax collector a detested traitor and instrument of oppression. However, this tax collector found favor with God because God seeks humility in all our approaches to him. In an age when self-esteem is highly valued we need reminding that Jesus preached, "Blessed are the meek."—Matthew 5:5.

Pharisees taught their students not to associate with tax collectors because they were often in contact with Gentiles and worked on the Sabbath. This made them ritually unclean. This is one reason why they despised Jesus. This tax collector stood at a distance. This signifies that he was conscious of his unworthiness and sinful condition and equally aware that God is holy. He stood at a distance because he recognized the immense distance between himself and God. He does not dare to look upward because he is ashamed of himself. His prayer was simple, "God be merciful to me, a sinner." He acknowledges his need of mercy. The Pharisee advertised his merit but the publican agonized for mercy and the outcome for both was completely different.

Spurgeon said, "The publican was the best theologian ~ for he prays like David of old." The events, which inspired David's great penitential prayer (Ps. 51), are adultery and murder. He gratified his lust by committing adultery with Bathsheba. He arranged the killing of her husband, Uriah, who was a loyal and able warrior in the King's army. Thus we read these words, straight from the broken heart of God's anointed servant who had sinned and is now sorrowing: "Have mercy on me, O God, according to your steadfast love; according to your abundant mercy blot out my transgressions." (Ps. 51:1) In the parable of the Pharisee and the Tax Collector Jesus sums up the message, "For everyone who exalts himself will be humbled, but the one who humbles himself will be exalted."—Luke 9:14.

APPENDIX 4 Tithing – A Case Study

One of the best ways to understand the principles of biblical interpretation is to take an issue and apply the principles to it in order to get a better understanding of that issue. Take, for example, the question "Is tithing biblical?" What does that question mean? It certainly features in Scripture but the question is really about whether or not it is applicable to believers today. Although they are related issues, there is nevertheless a difference between tithing and financial giving. Is tithing merely *described* in Scripture or is it *prescribed*? Is there a discernible pattern in Scripture? How are we to understand the whole issue of financial giving, especially when this topic is a sensitive one and one which is exploited by some greedy, unscrupulous and so-called "spiritual leaders" today?

The Widow's Offering (Mark 12:41-44)[123]

This is not a parable. This is a real person observed by Jesus and commended by him. The liberal giving of this woman contrasts with the greed of the teachers who "devour widow's houses." (Mk.12: 40). She gives all for the Lord as the Lord gave all for us. He gives to us with an open hand, an abundance of grace, mercy and kindness. He spared not his only Son. The setting is the court of women where both men and women were allowed to gather. This is where the temple treasury was located. Jesus sat down on a bench where he could watch people bring their offerings.

There were thirteen trumpet-shaped brass chests used for that purpose. It was not the rich with their large gifts which caught the Lord's attention but this poor widow. Widows were poor and vulnerable and exploited by many unscrupulous scribes. She donated two of the smallest coins in circulation in Palestine at that time. The widow's offering was greater in proportion as well as the spirit in which she gave. Jesus has something to say about the difference between superficial giving and sacrificial giving.

It is one thing to give in a formal manner out of a sense of obligation or duty but it is another thing entirely to give gladly. Giving should not be miserly, half-hearted or begrudging. Giving is an outward expression of inner faith. That is what giving to the work of the Lord is ~ an acknowledgement that all we have has come from his hand.

---

[123] Some of this is extracted from Kieran Beville, *Journey with Jesus through the Message of Mark*, (Cambridge, Ohio: Christian Publishing House, 2015). Used here with permission.

Those who understand the value of the work of God will give generously. God's people should always be prepared to give liberally, voluntarily and cheerfully. Each of these qualities should feature in every gift to God. We may volunteer to give, yet not be cheerful about it. When God is our vision, everything else pales into insignificance. The apostle Paul states clearly how God views giving, "...whoever sows sparingly will also reap sparingly, and whoever sows bountifully will also reap bountifully. Each one must give as he has decided in his heart, not reluctantly or under compulsion, for God loves a cheerful giver." (2 Cor. 9:6-7). Christians are exhorted to open-handed giving. There should be no compulsion from the church and there should be no reluctance from us when it comes to giving.

It is one thing to desire God's work to be done and even to pray fervently to that end but quite another thing to contribute financially to ensure that vision becomes a reality. It is the duty of all believers to support the work of the Lord. However, a word of caution is needed here. The believer must pray, pay and play! Making a financial contribution must not become a salve to our consciences. In giving we may be excusing ourselves from going ~ from playing our part in the work of God. That would be a bit like the wealthy being exempt from conscription in time of war. That may have been the case in some democracies but it has no place in the divine plan.

In the church today some people have substantial resources while others have very little. It is possible for wealthy people to be either generous or mean with what they have. The less well-off, however, are not invariably generous by nature. A person of limited means may be generous or have a miserly attitude. Meanness is probably less obvious in the case of the poorer person. It is wrong to make a virtue out of either poverty or wealth. The story of the widow's offering draws attention to something important in relation to giving. Jesus commends what some might condemn as foolish. She gave all she possessed. We might think that unless such a person develops a more sensible approach to money-management they will be trapped in poverty forever. But that is not what the Lord says. Jesus said: "Truly, I say to you." Jesus always told the truth, but whenever he uses this phrase he is asking his disciples (then and now) to pay particular attention to the truth being taught.

What exactly is the truth being emphasized here? I believe that what Jesus wants us to get hold of is this ~ there is a vast difference between superficial and sacrificial giving. This widow did not give from a surplus. There is nothing balanced or budgeted about her giving. It is not affordable. In fact, one could say it appears reckless. However, it reflects an attitude of total love and deep faith. There was nothing shallow or partial in the way she gave. Giving must never be tokenism dressed up as thanks.

It is a sad fact of life that wealth is a serious obstacle to true spirituality. Whether wealth is amassed through honest or dishonest means, one often finds that making money is the chief aim of wealthy people. It is something to which they may have dedicated their lives ~ a single-minded ambition, a number-one priority. Such self-made men and women are often proud and self-sufficient. They are confident in their own resources and, sadly, arrogant. These people are often the chiefs and bosses of their own commercial empires. They find it difficult to be humble. In the church they sometimes find it difficult to follow, because they are not used to being led. Of course, the Holy Spirit can transform such people into what all of us should be ~ generous to those in need and willing and joyful supporters of the Lord's work. A wealthy believer can make a significant contribution to the work of the local church. But even in doing this there is a danger that he sees himself as the paymaster and expects to call the shots. However, the idea that "he who pays the piper calls the tune" has no place in the church of Christ.

It should be remembered that God does not need our money to accomplish his purposes. Rather, he desires our cheerful willingness to give sacrificially rather than superficially. This is the biblical perspective, which needs to be preached without fear or favor. Sometimes those who can afford to contribute to a particular need say things like, "I don't want to encourage idleness" or "I wouldn't like to create false expectations." They might argue that money won't make any real difference and what is really required is better financial management and budgeting skills. On the face of it this kind of reasoning makes sense because there is a good deal of truth in it. However, we need to be more compassionate than critical. Those who value money more than anything else are reluctant to part with it. We can rationalize our rationing but God expects us to give generously.

God is Generous

In the temple, Jesus observed what people were giving and he still does. He sees the motives, the excuses and the sacrifice. One very good reason for showing generosity is that God himself is generous by nature. If we desire to be truly like him, then we should not neglect to be generous. God's generosity is most evident in his willingness to cancel our great debt of sin. It is in the context of our own giving that Paul writes, "For you know the grace of our Lord Jesus Christ, that though he was rich, yet for your sake he became poor, so that you by his poverty might become rich." (2 Cor. 8:9) The ledger has been balanced because he paid the price

167

in full. Luke records the thinking of Jesus on this issue, "...give, and it will be given to you. Good measure, pressed down, shaken together, running over, will be put into your lap. For with the measure you use it will be measured back to you." (Lk. 6:38) He pours a quart into a pint pot. Paul prays that the Ephesians "...may be filled with all the fullness of God." (Eph. 3:19) Inevitably, such filling will result in overflowing.

The Rich Young Ruler

The rich young ruler had done everything required by the Law, but he was unwilling to sell all that he had and give it to the poor. (Mt. 19:16-22) Ultimately, money meant more to him than obedience to the Master. Jesus could read his heart and knew how to touch the central issue. Some might suggest that Jesus' demands are unreasonable and that few of us would be prepared to follow him on these terms. But unless we are prepared to do whatever Christ asks of us we cannot count ourselves as his disciples at all. When we consider the fact that the Lord loved us and spared not his only Son how can we ever give too much? The tithe seems a small offering of thanks. When we consider the quality of God's love and his giving, it leaves us speechless and awestruck. These words capture something of how wonderful God's giving love really is:

The Love of God

Could we with ink the ocean fill,
And were the skies of parchment made,
Were every stalk on earth a quill,
And every man a scribe by trade;
To write the love of God above
Would drain the ocean dry;
Nor could the scroll contain the whole,
Though stretched from sky to sky.[124]

Money matters

Money is a sensitive subject. Money is essential. We depend upon it to provide the necessities of life. Money is important, but the world places too much emphasis on it. Money can be used for good ~ to provide for the needs of the kingdom of God, but it can be destructive. Paul told Timothy that, "the love of money is a root of all kinds of evils." (1 Tim. 6:10) The writer to the Hebrews said, "Keep your life free from love of money, and be content with what you have." (Heb. 13:5) Money

---

[124] Frederick M. Lehman, 1917. This third verse is by Rabbi Mayer, 1096, which was anonymously altered. It was penciled on the wall of a room in an insane asylum by a patient. The profound lines were discovered when they laid him in his coffin.

must be used properly. Christians have a responsibility to use the resources given to them by God to further God's kingdom upon the earth. When God's people returned from seventy years of exile in Babylon they rebuilt the temple under the leadership of Ezra and Nehemiah, "Some of the heads of families, when they came to the house of the LORD that is in Jerusalem, made freewill offerings for the house of God, to erect it on its site. According to their ability they gave to the treasury of the work..."—Ezra 2:68-69.

We too have been delivered from captivity, and we have a duty and the privilege of building for God. When we invest our money in the kingdom of God, we also place our hearts there. When we invest our finances in the world, we tie our affections to things below and not things above. Jesus said:

> Do not lay up for yourselves treasures on earth, where moth and rust destroy and where thieves break in and steal, but lay up for yourselves treasures in heaven, where neither moth nor rust destroys and where thieves do not break in and steal. For where your treasure is, there your heart will be also....No one can serve two masters, for either he will hate the one and love the other, or he will be devoted to the one and despise the other. You cannot serve God and money"—Matthew 6:19-24.

Money can lead to terrible bondage, "The rich rules over the poor, and the borrower is the slave of the lender." (Prov. 22:7) If we allow ourselves to fall into the slavery of debt, we are hindering our ability to follow the Lord properly. Often, our indebtedness prevents us from serving the Lord as he would have us serve. Money should be used to bring glory to God. When money is properly used to glorify the Lord, then the Lord will prove his power to provide for his people, "Bring the full tithe into the storehouse...And thereby put me to the test, says the LORD of hosts, if I will not open the windows of heaven for you and pour down for you a blessing until there is no more need." (Mal. 3:8-11) When God is denied this opportunity, then the child of God has forfeited a great blessing.

Giving is a spiritual act. In this passage about the widow's offering Jesus observed people contributing their money to the temple treasury. Jesus is still watching people give. What would he say about our giving? There are sins of commission and sins of omission. Sin is not just the bad things we do it is also the good things we fail to do, "So whoever knows the right thing to do and fails to do it, for him it is sin."—James 4:17.

Tithing

Abram commenced tithing when he gave Melchizedek (priest/king) a tenth of everything. Jacob continued it. Jacob resolved to give a tithe (a tenth), "And of all that you give me I will give a full tenth to you" (Gen. 28:22). Malachi commanded it, "Bring the full tithe into the storehouse, that there may be food in my house. And thereby put me to the test…if I will not open the windows of heaven for you and pour down for you a blessing until there is no more need." (Mal. 3:10). Jesus condoned it, "Woe to you, scribes and Pharisees, hypocrites! For you tithe mint and dill and cumin and have neglected the weightier matters of the law: justice and mercy and faithfulness. These you ought to have done, without neglecting the others." (Mt. 23:23) So tithing was commenced by Abram, continued by Jacob, commanded by Malachi and condoned by Christ. It was also commended by Paul, "On the first day of every week, each of you is to put something aside and store it up, as he may prosper, so that there will be no collecting when I come."—1 Corinthians 16:2.

We cannot say that tithing (a tenth) is commanded in Scripture and binding on believers. However, it is clear from this that some form of continuous giving applies to Christians. This is one of the easiest places to neglect our duty, but it is also one of the most practical areas to prove our faith. We cannot fail to notice the promise of God in Malachi to those who give to God. We cannot fail to notice how God rewarded Jacob, "…for with only my staff I crossed this Jordan, and now I have become two camps." (Gen. 32:10) There is an inescapable pattern here. But many preachers are afraid to preach it because of some who have distorted the truth in what has come to be known as, "the prosperity gospel."

The Matter, Manner, and Measure of Giving

Jesus condemned the superficial giving of some when he commended the sacrificial giving of the widow's offering. We do not give in order to gain. We do not give to God because he is needy. We give in thankfulness for his faithfulness. There are some basic reasons why people do not tithe. Some people simply do not understand the place that giving holds in the lives of believers. Some simply refuse to obey the Lord and do not give even though they know they should.

God has a rightful claim to our resources. All that we have belongs to God. It is not just ten percent that belongs to God it is one-hundred-percent. We need to examine ourselves about the *matter*, the *manner* and the *measure* of our giving. As the metal coins were cast into these trumpets, they made a loud noise and the more money that was cast in, the louder the sound. Those who wanted to put on a show could easily do so. This was a practice that was condemned by Jesus:

> "Thus, when you give to the needy, sound no trumpet before you, as the hypocrites do in the synagogues and in the streets, that they may be praised by others. Truly, I say to you, they have received their reward. But when you give to the needy, do not let your left hand know what your right hand is doing, so that your giving may be in secret. And your Father who sees in secret will reward you."—Matthew 6:2.

When the widow gave her two small coins, they sounded small compared to the offerings of the rich. But this widow's testimony still stands as a great example of sacrificial giving. The tithe is a fair way of giving proportionately. We do not all give the same sum of money but the same percentage, and it is sanctified by the Lord, "Every tithe of the land, whether of the seed of the land or of the fruit of the trees, is the LORD's; it is holy to the LORD."—Leviticus 27:30.

Tithing did not originate with the Law. Abel brought the Lord the first-fruits of his flocks (Gen. 4:4). Four-hundred-and-thirty years before the Law was given Abraham offered the Lord a tithe of all his increase (Gen. 14:20). We are not to give only when we have a windfall or some excess or unexpected bonanza. We are not to give only out of guilt ~ out of conviction, yes! People who give out of a sense of guilt stop doing so when the feeling of guilt stops. If you are wondering whether the tithe (ten percent) refers to gross pay (before tax and other deductions) or net pay (after tax and other deductions), I can't help you there. Ask the Lord about it.

We are to give of our first-fruits. When we make the first part holy, then the rest becomes holy as well, "If the dough offered as firstfruits is holy, so is the whole lump, and if the root is holy, so are the branches." (Rom. 11:16). When we tithe, we are declaring that everything else belongs to the Lord as well. We are to consider not just the *matter* of giving (i.e. the fact that we should give) we are also to consider the *manner* of our giving (i.e. cheerfully). But we must also consider our motives. The trumpets must have sounded very impressive when a large donation was given. They impressed men, but the widow's offering impressed the Lord. It is not the sum of money that makes the offering worthy. It is the heart of the giver. We should give from thankful hearts. We should give cheerfully, "God loves a cheerful giver." (2 Cor. 9:7). We should give liberally. We are not to be stingy when it comes to giving to the Lord's work or his people.

God blesses us in proportion to the level of our giving. I know that might sound controversial but, "...whoever sows sparingly will also reap sparingly, and whoever sows bountifully will also reap bountifully." (2 Cor. 9:6). The context of this verse is financial giving. Remember Jesus said, "...give, and it will be given to you. Good measure, pressed down, shaken together, running over, will be put into your lap. For with the measure you use it will be measured back to you."—Luke 6:38.

There will be some who will protest that they cannot afford to give. That is not true! Regardless of what comes into our lives, we can always give. We cannot afford *not* to give. We should give sacrificially. If you wait to start giving until you have plenty, you will face two problems. First, you might never get to where you think you have plenty. Second, if you do have extra, it will seem like too much to give. The rich gave out of their surplus, but the widow gave all that she had. That got the Lord's attention! It still does!

RECOMMENDED READING AND RESOURCES

Allis, Oswald T. *Prophecy and the Church* (Wipf & Stock, 2001).

Archer, Gleason L. *Encyclopedia of Bible Difficulties* (Grand Rapids: Zondervan, 1982).

Barr, David L. *New Testament Story*, (Wadsworth Publishing, 1995)

Bauer, Walter (Author), Frederick William Danker (Editor). *A Greek-English Lexicon of the New Testament and Other Early Christian Literature* (3rd edition, University of Chicago Press, 2001).

Berkhof, Louis. *Principles of Biblical Interpretation* (Grand Rapids, Michigan: Baker Book House, 1950).

Beville, Kieran. *Journey with Jesus through the Message of Mark*, (Cambridge, Ohio, Christian Publishing House, 2015).

Blaiklock, E. M. *The Acts of the Apostles: An Historical Commentary* (London: Tyndale, 1959).

Bridges, Charles. *A Commentary on Ecclesiastes*, (Geneva Series, Banner of Truth, 1960)

Bruce F. F. *Paul: Apostle of the Free Spirit* (rev. ed.; Carlisle: Paternoster, 1992).

Bruce F.F. *New Testament History* (Galilee / Doubleday; Reissue edition, 1980).

Bruce, F. F. *New Testament Development of Old Testament Themes* (Wipf & Stock, 2004).

Carson, D.A. *Exegetical Fallacies* (Grand Rapids: Baker, 1984).

Cole, Alan. Exodus, *Tyndale Old Testament Commentaries*, (Downer's Grove, IL: InterVarsity, 1973).

Coogan, Michael D. The Old Testament, a Historical and Literary Introduction to the Hebrew Scriptures (Oxford University Press, 2005).

Dodd C. H. *The Parables of the Kingdom*, (New York: Charles Scribner's Sons; Revised edition, 1961).

Duvall, J. Scott, and J. Daniel Hays. *Grasping God's Word: A Hands on Approach to Reading, Interpreting, and Applying the Bible* (Grand Rapids, Mich.: Zondervan, 2001).

Edersheim, Alfred. Bible History: *Old Testament*, (Hendrickson, updated edition, 1995).

Elwell, Walter A. Evangelical Dictionary of Theology, (Grand Rapids, Michigan: Baker Book House, 1984).

Farnell, F. David, Edward D. Andrews, Thomas Howe, Thomas Marshall, Benjamin Cocar, and Dianna Newman. *Basics of Biblical Criticism: Helpful or Harmful?* [Second Edition] (Cambridge, OH: Christian Publishing House, 2016).

Ferguson, Sinclair B; David F Wright, J. I. Packer. *New Dictionary of Theology.* (Downers Grove, Ill.: InterVarsity Press, 1988).

Geisler, Norman L. and William E. Nix. *A General Introduction to the Bible*, (Revised and Expanded. Chicago, IL: Moody, 1996).

Geisler, Norman L. and Thomas Howe. *The Big Book of Bible Difficulties: Clear and Concise Answers from Genesis to Revelation* (Grand Rapids, MI: Baker Books, 2008).

Geisler, Norman L. and Bill Roach. *Defending Inerrancy: Affirming the Accuracy of Scripture for a New Generation* (Grand Rapids, MI: Baker Books, 2011).

Grenz, Stanley J., David Guretzki & Cherith Fee Nordling. *Pocket Dictionary of Theological Terms* (Downers Grove, IL: InterVarsity Press, 1999).

Haley, John. *Alleged Discrepancies of the Bible*, (Whitaker House; updated edition, 2004).

Hartill, J E. *Principles of Biblical Hermeneutics*, (Grand Rapids, Michigan: Zondervan, 1960).

Hendricks, Howard G., William D. D. Hendricks. *Living By the Book: The Art and Science of Reading the Bible* (Chicago: Moody Press, 1992).

Hodge Charles. *Systematic Theology 1*, (Peabody: Hendrickson, 2003).

Hoekema, Anthony. *The Bible and the Future*, (Wm. B. Eerdmans, 1994).

Jamieson, Fausset and Brown. *Commentary on the Whole Bible*, Vol. IV, (Zondervan, 1999).

Kaiser, Walter C. *A History of Israel: From the Bronze Age Through the Jewish Wars*, (Broadman & Holman, 1998).

Kaiser, Walter C. and Moisés Silva. *An Introduction to Biblical Hermeneutics: The Search for Meaning*, (Rev. ed. Grand Rapids, Mich.: Zondervan, 2007).

Kaiser, Walter. F.F. Bruce, Manfred Brauch, Peter Davids, *Hard Sayings of the Bible* (Downers Grove, IL: Inter-Varsity Press, 1996).

Kidner, Derek. *The Message of Ecclesiastes*, (IVP Academic, reprint edition, 1984).

La Rondelle, Hans K. *The Israel of God in Prophecy: Principles of Prophetic Interpretation* (Andrews University Press, 1983).

Lewis, Johnson, S. *The Old Testament in the New: An Argument for Biblical Inspiration Contemporary Evangelical Perspectives*, (Zondervan, 1980).

McCartney, Dan & Charles Clayton, *Let the Reader Understand: A Guide to Interpreting and Applying the Bible* (Wheaton, IL: Victor Books, 1994).

McQuilkin, Robertson. *Understanding and Applying the Bible* (Chicago: Moody Press, Rev. edition 1992).

Mickelsen, A. Berkeley. *Interpreting the Bible* (Grand Rapids, Michigan: Eerdmans, 1963).

O'Brien, David E. *Today's Handbook for Solving Bible Difficulties* (Minneapolis: Bethany House Publishers, 1990).

Packer, J. I. *God Has Spoken: Revelation and the Bible* (Baker Academic, 1994).

Ramm, Bernard. *Protestant Biblical Interpretation: A Textbook of Hermeneutics*, (3rd edition, Grand Rapids, Mich.: Baker Book House, 1970).

Thomas, Robert L. and F. David Farnell. *THE JESUS CRISIS The Inroads of Historical Criticism into Evangelical Scholarship* (Grand Rapids, MI: Kregel Academic & Professional, 1998)

Thomas, Robert L. *Evangelical Hermeneutics: The New Versus the Old* (Grand Rapids, MI: Kregel Academic & Professional, 2002)

Sire, James. *Scripture Twisting: 20 Ways the Cults Misread the Bible*, (IVP, 1980).

Sproul, R.C. *Knowing Scripture* (Downers Grove, IL: Inter-Varsity Press, 1977).

Stein, Robert H. *A Basic Guide to Interpreting the Bible: Playing by the Rules* (Baker Academic; 2 edition, 2011).

Stein, Robert H. *Difficult Passages in the Gospels*, (Grand Rapids: Baker, 1984).

Stein, Robert H. *Difficult Passages in the New Testament: Interpreting Puzzling Texts in the Gospels and Epistles* (Grand Rapids: Baker Book House, 1990).

Stott, John R. W. *Baptism and Fullness: The Work of the Holy Spirit Today* (2nd ed.; Leicester: Inter-Varsity Press, 1975).

Tate, W. Randolph. *Biblical Interpretation: An Integrated Approach* (Rev. ed. Peabody, Mass.: Hendrickson Pub., 1997).

Terry Milton S. *Biblical Hermeneutics: a Treatise on the Interpretation of the Old and New Testaments* (Grand Rapids, Michigan: Zondervan, 1974).

Thistleton, Anthony. *New Horizons in Hermeneutics* (Grand Rapids, Michigan: Zondervan, 1992).

Virkler, Henry A. *Hermeneutics: Principles and Processes of Biblical Interpretation,* (Baker Academic, 2007).

Webb, William J. *Slaves, Women and Homosexuals: Exploring the Hermeneutics of Cultural Analysis* (Authentic Media, 2002).

Zuck Roy B. *Basic Bible Interpretation,* (David C. Cook, 1991).

Bibliography

Allis, Oswald T. *Prophecy and the Church*. Eugene: Wipf & Stock, 2001.

Andrews, Edward D. *OVERCOMING BIBLE DIFFICULTIES: Answers to the So-Called Errors and Contradictions*. Cambridge: Christian Publishing House, 2015.

Archer, Gleason L. *Encyclopedia of Bible Difficulties*. Grand Rapids: Zondervan, 1982.

Arndt, William, Frederick W. Danker, and Walter Bauer. *A Greek-English Lexicon of the New Testament and Other Early Christian Literature. 3rd ed.* . Chicago: University of Chicago Press, 2000.

Barr, David L. *New Testament Story*. Independence: Wadsworth Publishing, 1995.

Berkhof, Louis. *Principles of Biblical Interpretation*. Grand Rapids, MI: Baker Book House, 1994.

Blaiklock, E. M. *The Acts of the Apostles: An Historical Commentary*. London: Tyndale, 1959.

Bridges, Charles. *A Commentary on Ecclesiastes, (Geneva Series of Commentaries)*. Waikato: Titus Books, 2013.

Bruce, F. F. *New Testament Development of Old Testament Themes*. Eugene: Wipf & Stock, 2004.

—. *Paul: Apostle of the Heart Set Free*. Grand Rapids: Eerdmans, 1977.

Bruce, F. F. *The New Testament Documents: Are they Reliable?* Downer Groves: Inter Varsity, 1981.

Charles, R. H. *Revelation, The International Critical Commentary, Vol. 1*. Edinburgh: T & T Clark, 1906.

Cole, Alan. *Exodus, Tyndale Old Testament Commentaries*. Downers Grove: InterVarsity, 1973.

Dodd, C. H. *The Parables of the Kingdom, (Revised edition)*. New York: Charles Scribner's Sons, 1961.

Elwell, Walter A. *Baker Encyclopedia of the Bible*. Grand Rapids: Baker Book House, 1988.

—. *Evangelical Dictionary of Theology (Second Edition)*. Grand Rapids: Baker Academic, 2001.

Farrar, F. W. *The Messages of the Books*. Charleston: Nabu Press, 2010.

Fausset, A. R., and David Brown. *Jamieson, Fausset, and Brown's Commentary On the Whole Bible, Vol. IV, (, 1999.* Grand Rapids: Zondervan, 1999.

Fee, Gordon D., and Douglas Stuart. *How to Read the Bible for All Its Worth.* Grand Rapids: Zondervan, 1981, 1993, 2003.

Goodspeed, Edgar. *Modern Apocrypha: Famous "Biblical" Hoaxes.* Boston: Beacon Press, 1956.

Grenz, Stanley J., David Guretzki, and Cherith Fee Nordling. *Pocket Dictionary of Theological Terms.* Downers Grove: InterVarsity Press, 1999.

Hagner, Donald A. *"The Old Testament in the New Testament," Interpreting the Word of God, (eds. Samuel J. Schultz & Morris A. Inch).* Chicago: Moody Press, 1976.

Hendricks, Howard G. *Living by the Book.* Chicago: Moody Press, 1991.

Hodge, Charles. *Systematic Theology 1.* Peabody: Hendrickson, 2003.

Hoekema, Anthony. *The Bible and the Future.* Grand Rapids: Wm. B. Eerdmans, 1994.

Johnson, S. Lewis. *The Old Testament in the New: An Argument for Biblical Inspiration Contemporary Evangelical Perspectives.* Grand Rapids: Zondervan, 1980.

Kaiser, Walter C., and Moises Silva. *Introduction to Biblical Hermeneutics: The Search for Meaning.* Grand Rapids: Zondervan, 1994, 2007.

Kidner, Derek. *The Message of Ecclesiastes (reprint edition).* Downers Grove: IVP Academic, 1984.

LaSor, William. *"Interpretation of Prophecy," Hermeneutics, Bernard Ramm.* Grand Rapids: Baker, 1971.

McQuilkin, Robertson. *Understanding and Applying the Bible (Rev. edition).* Chicago: Moody Press, 1992.

Murray, H. *The Life of Arthur W. Pink.* Edinburgh: Banner of Truth, 2004.

Osborne, Grant R. *THE HERMENEUTICAL SPIRAL A Comprehensive Introduction to Biblical Interpretation (2nd Edition).* Downers Grove, IL: InterVarsity Press, 2006.

Packer, J. I. *God Has Spoken: Revelation and the Bible.* Grand Rapids: Baker Academic, 1994.

Pinnock, Clark. *Biblical Revelation.* Grand Rapids: Baker, 1973.

Ramm, Bernard. *Protestant Biblical Interpretation: A Textbook of Hermeneutics, 3rd rev. ed.* Grand Rapids, MI: Baker, 1999.

Rondelle, Hans K. La. *The Israel of God in Prophecy: Principles of Prophetic Interpretation.* Berrien Springs: Andrews University Press, 1983.

Sire, James. *Scripture Twisting: 20 Ways the Cults Misread the Bible, (IVP, 1980.* Downers Grove: InterVarsity Press, 1980.

Stein, Robert H. *A Basic Guide to Interpreting the Bible: Playing by the Rules.* Grand Rapids: Baker Books, 1994.

—. *Difficult Passages in the Gospels.* Grand Rapids: Baker, 1984.

Stott, John R. W. *Baptism and Fullness: The Work of the Holy Spirit Today (2nd ed).* Leicester: Inter-Varsity Press, 1975.

Terry, Milton S. *Biblical Hermeneutics: A Treatise on the Interpretation of the Old and New Testaments.* Grand Rapids: Zondervan, 1974.

Virkler, Henry A, and Karelynne Gerber Ayayo. *Hermeneutics: Principles and Processes of Biblical Interpretation.* Grand Rapids, MI: Baker Academic, 1981, 2007.

Yamauchi, Edwin M. ""The Word From Nag Hammadi"." *Christianity Today*, January 1978: 19.

Zuck, Roy B. *Basic Bible Interpretation: A Prafctical Guide to Discovering Biblical Truth.* Colorado Springs: David C. Cook, 1991.

SUBJECT INDEX

Made in United States
North Haven, CT
12 October 2023

42670539R00118